Leadership Secrets for Care Home Managers

To achieve a CQC rating of "good" to "outstanding" by ensuring your care home is "well-led" and "effective".

Liam Palmer

Copyright © 2018 Liam Palmer

All rights reserved, including the right to reproduce this book, or portions thereof in any form. No part of this text may be reproduced, transmitted, downloaded, decompiled, reverse engineered, or stored, in any form or introduced into any information storage and retrieval system, in any form or by any means, whether electronic or mechanical without the express written permission of the author.

ISBN: 978-1-326-63312-7

PublishNation
www.publishnation.co.uk

Dedicated to the carers. Your dedication makes it all possible.

Introduction to new book "Leadership secrets for Care Home Managers."

We cannot solve our problems with the same thinking we used when we created them." Albert Einstein

This book is a follow on from my first book "**Management Development for Care and Nursing Home Managers**", a compilation of 16 peer reviewed articles with the book initially released in June 2016. This new book published in October 2018 includes 15 new peer reviewed articles. It has been just under 4 years since that first article. Inevitably the themes and concepts have developed and matured. I hope they will be of use to you. As we apply the quote from Einstein, to truly solve some of the challenges in social care, we often need a new type of thinking. Many of the articles that follow are based on this type of reasoning.

I recently watched the 2014 movie "The Imitation Game", starring Benedict Cumberbatch as the World War two Code Breaker, Alan Turing. His work led to cracking the enigma code to decipher German communications during this period and shortened the war. The impact of his deductive thinking lives on through modern computing. What struck me most about the movie was the striking clarity of how he defined the problem and his sense of certainty of where the solution lay. As someone who has also spent most of his time "in his own world", on the fringes of the mainstream, his success as an unconventional thinker continues to inspires me.

Background to the first book

After moving into private care home management in 2013, I was surprised by the disconnect between expectations and the reality of working in social care. There was the public **and the regulator** (CQC) expectations of higher standards and then there were the team tasked with delivering these ever higher standards. These managers had deep experience as carers and nurses but often lacked access to leadership training to develop higher level skills (influencing, communications, lateral thinking) to deliver sustainable quality. In addition to this, their primary tools are often paper records that are manually cross-referenced!

Despite these under-developed fundamentals, there's something mysterious and affirming about working in care. This book is a modest effort to define some of those challenges in running a care home and how I recommend responding to them. I wrote firstly to share with my peers and secondly as a means of introducing home managers in how to think and operate like a leader.

Between the first book (June 2016 and now autumn 2018)

Considering the first book had a tagline (2nd heading) of "equipping home managers to raise care and quality standards", it seemed an obvious choice to contact the UK regulator for some sort of endorsement. It took me a year of letter writing to eventually meet Andrea Sutcliffe CBE, the Chief Inspector of Social Care for the CQC. The offices are off Buckingham Palace Road in Central London. I was elated and nervous. I expected to meet someone who was like a God in the form of a bureaucrat. I was in for a surprise. Andrea was effortlessly charming, very human, bright and an extraordinary leader. She displayed a deep sense of empathy about the importance of good care. She graciously put up with my incoherent ramble before offering some introductions and advice. Fortunately for me, the findings of my book mirrored those of her inspection teams. We agreed that good leadership, reflected by "well led" and "effective ratings" were linked with having a quality service. Leadership was key!

Process of writing

Each article was previously published via the "www.linked-in.com" professional platform, eventually to a social care audience of around 12,500 people. The feedback and comments developed my thinking – I am grateful for all who interacted with me.

Often the theme or challenge would sit with me, sometimes for a year, sometimes longer as I mulled over the key points. I wanted to provide a narrative that was empowering that said to managers whilst we can't control all the factors around us, we can influence some, we can all strive for care driven by compassion.

The content is based on principles and lessons that I checked myself and discussed with my peers prior to releasing. By insisting on mastering a topic before writing on it, it made the process of writing slow but the output more authentic. In a world dominated by social media and short attention spans, it is hard to determine sources of information that are worthy of our attention. I aspired to create content that is worthy of someone's time. If I've made you think differently about some of these challenges and problems, my work is complete.

Thank you

Liam Palmer

Birmingham, September 2018

Foreword to "Leadership Secrets for Care Home Managers".

Liam and I worked together on a consultancy project for a struggling home and we developed a rapport easily - finding common ground as values based professionals, focusing on integrity, honesty and a no excuses approach to achieving quality for those in our care. We both share a passion for better care and weren't willing to compromise on these values.

Delivering a care experience that is considered to be "good" or "outstanding" according to the CQC regulations I helped develop can be a complex undertaking but worthwhile. In these pages Liam advocates a trust based, pragmatic leadership approach drawing on various disciplines to find an approach that works. His passion is evident and he cares equally about his team as he does his residents and always strives to offer solutions to these sometimes complex dynamics.

If you are wanting to develop a culture of quality, staff engagement and a sense of excellence for your home, I think you will find some gold within these pages.

Barry Stanley-Wilkinson

Ex CQC lawyer and co-creator of CQC regulations

October 2018

Contents

Part 1 – Masterclass in Management

1.1 Care Home Manager – best job in the world? — Pg 7

1.2 "There's no place like home!" (Dorothy, Wizard of Oz). — Pg 11

1.3 Staff engagement / are we missing something? — Pg 15

1.4 Got problem staff? What they need is a good..? — Pg 19

1.5 Developing your team – Part 1 – under-pinning theory — Pg 23

1.6 Developing your team – Part 2 – in practice — Pg 27

Part 2 – Masterclass in Home Leadership

2.1 High levels of Care Home Manager attrition — Pg 37

2.2 Care Home Manager - who leads best.. — Pg 43

2.3 Facing the "agency problem" in UK care homes — Pg 47

2.4 Moving forward with the "agency problem" — Pg 51

2.5 How to take charge of a challenged home — Pg 55

Part 3 – Masterclass in Leadership Qualities

3.1 **Empathy** – Having a "bad" day — Pg 67

3.2 **Gratitude** – what could be more beautiful — Pg 71

3.3 **Flexibility** – How I made a change — Pg 75

3.4 **Persistence** – when all seems lost — Pg 79

3.5 **Inspiration** – what inspires you to do the work you do? — Pg 83

Part 4

4.1 What is the cost…of having a "revolving door" for home managers? **Pg 93**

4.2 With the "revolving door" ..do you want to break the pattern? **Pg 97**

4.3 Beware! The greatest risk in your Care Home/….facility today! **Pg 103**

4.4 Managing the "greatest risk in your care home" today **Pg 107**

4.5 ..Home Manager – ..best job in the world! Reflections 2 years on. **Pg 111**

Part 5

5.1 Home Manager / Breaking the taboo on d****. **Pg 121**

5.2 Care Home Manager - leadership secrets for CONSISTENT success - identifying the one key personal quality we all need. **Pg 125**

5.3 Dear boss, my commitment to you was lost today. This is why… **Pg 129**

5.4 Dear boss, working for you is affecting my health. This is why… **Pg 133**

5.5 Dear boss, working in this organisation is affecting my MENTAL HEALTH. This is why… **Pg 137**

5.6 Care Home Manager / how much better is a CQC rated "outstanding" home?. Reflections from 2 visits in December. **Pg 141**

Part 6

6.1 …Manager accountability - legal vs organisational. Never the t..? **Pg 151**

6.2 Care Home Manager / why you shouldn't be frightened of the "S" word / tips for building your private bed occupancy. **Pg 155**

6.3 Care Home Manager / which services can be turned and which can't? Reflections from supporting an owner / operator. **Pg 161**

6.4 .. Home Manager / .. is it time you had that difficult conversation? **Pg 165**

6.5 Care Home Manager / vocation vs job / seeing the "giants" in our midst **Pg 169**

Part 1 – Masterclass in Management

Part 1 – Masterclass in Management - overview

In this series of articles, we take a new look at some familiar themes and beliefs – firstly looking at seeing a care home manager as the best job in the world and I made my case for this.

We move on to examining the importance of home and having empathy for those in our care. I look at judgements we can all make and how they can be wrong.

I look at a core theme in care at the moment – staff engagement and take a radical view as to why levels are not where they might be.

Next we look at a core belief I came across in care – the "problem staff" and I review this assessment with a twist.

Lastly, for me, delivering great care consistently will always be through the team. What if we don't have an established team – how do you make it established and function? I introduce a model (Myers Briggs) for you to proactively develop your care home team.

Part 1 – Masterclass in Management   Pg

1.1 Care Home Manager – best job in the world?   7

1.2 There's no place like home! (Dorothy, Wizard of Oz)   11

1.3 Staff engagement / are we missing something?   15

1.4 Got problem staff? What they need is a good..?   19

1.5 Developing your team – Part 1 – under-pinning theory 23

1.6 Developing your team – Part 2 – in practice   27

1.1 Care Home Manager - best job in the world?

It has been a year since I moved to a private care provider working with older people after working as a senior manager in a large private hospital and 6 months since I took up the reins of a 79 bed residential home. I was equally excited and apprehensive about the move and the possibilities for working in this sector. I had never considered "care" before - my thoughts influenced by a jumble sale in an old people's home as a child, seeing a few people with Alzheimer's in a hospital and then of course the scare stories in the media of neglect and what sounded like a scary place to work.

When I took up the reins of my first home, I saw those suffering with dementia and went to see them every day - for a while my heart sunk, I am a big-hearted person and have a sweet spot for older people but still, the reality and tragedy of their pain and loss hit me hard, I wondered, did I have enough heart to love these people every day, keep pushing for the very best for them? After a few months, these people came alive to me, we started to get to know each other even if no words were shared, we have our jokes, smiles, habits - I became the "young man with the big smile - always smiling" according to several of these lovely older ladies that stay with us. I am happy with that - if my smile gives them happiness, well it is not much, but it is something.

Several precious memories of my work in care over the last year care come from 2 particular residents;

One who told me about her husband of 50 years - "best man I ever met, never a cross word, he made me laugh" she was still praising him years after he passed. She had dementia - was her memory being overly sentimental I wondered? I got to know her a bit - she was a remarkable lady and I think she was telling the truth. What an inspiration - to live in such a way that your wife still praises you after you passed - amazing lady! I hope to visit her in Cambridge next week.

Secondly, a lady in my dementia unit said "You are very handsome and you are lovely, I am not just saying that, I really mean it" she said looking in my eyes. She said that "Your mother must be so proud of you." Whether it is true is irrelevant, at that moment, this lady meant it, said it with such conviction. I could have cried. Nicest thing anyone had ever said to me. A precious moment.

There are times where the risks inherent in the role of care home manager can be pressing, it is by no means a job for the faint-hearted but with a degree of autonomy as registered manager and the help and support of a great staff team, nearly anything is possible.

Care Home Manager - best job in the world? I think so.

(Also see updated article 4.5 on page 111)

1.1 Reflective practice on **Care Home Manager – best job in the world?**

Key themes covered

Person centred care, joy in service, precious moments from those with work with.

What does this article mean to you?

What can / would you apply from this learning to your practice?

Other notes

1.2 "There's no place like home!" (Dorothy, Wizard of Oz) What does home mean to you?

This reflection came after sharing a moment with a lady who lives in the dementia wing of our care home. It got me thinking and if I am really honest, upset me a bit. The link with Dorothy (in the movie above - 1939) will become clear a bit later - bear with me.

As I do one of my daily walks around the home sharing and smiling with those living in this community, this lady would look distressed if I came within 10 feet of her and say "go away – I don't like you." Fair enough, I thought! After, she even tried to hit me a few times in frustration. She would shake my hand initially then pull my arm in till it hurt. Later we agreed for her to try being more gentle. She meant no harm and was simply reaching out for attention in her own way.

More recently, after she had injured her arm, she reached out to hold my hand. I took it. I later checked she was getting her pain relief and made extra checks on her well-being, giving her some reassurance about the wound healing on her arm. She would look at me, hold my hand for 10 seconds or so, feel that care and then let go. It worked and I was happy she felt understood and supported.

I saw her yesterday; her bottom lip was shaking. I bent down and offered my hand. She took both. She was fearful and wanted to go home. She asked how to get home - "I don't know, I don't know" she said, clearly very distressed. It seemed like her heart was breaking. It reminded me of Dorothy in the Wizard of Oz yearning for home. She asked me not to leave. Distressed, she pulled me in. I pulled back slightly, weary of being hit and yet it was a desire to pull me close. I felt embarrassed that I thought to protect myself from a slap and instead it was an embrace! Later when she calmed and I left, I found a female carer to give her more physical reassurance.

The whole episode made me think – how would it feel if I could never go home? This lady had enjoyed her own home for all her life, a garden with complete control and choice and here she was now sharing a living room with many "strangers". Perhaps that what it was for her, a memory of the feeling of home and that if she goes back, everything will be ok.

Whilst I will never know understand her feelings exactly, (this lady is partially verbal), I can take a guess that it was the same need we all have– to have a refuge from the outside world, where we are understood, loved, safe and secure. A place where we are known, of shared memories, familiarity – where we matter. For anybody, needing to give up their home and embracing a care home community is a big step, it often works beautifully, but at best it is a replacement home for the one given up. At times, for that very reason it will fall short of that individual's expectations.

Today, that feeling resonates me. I feel it keenly. What can I do to make this place feel like home for all who live here? We can foster a culture of a close knit, high morale team with a family feel. We can continually strive for high standards and encourage keen observation and personalized care and remind staff that what these people want and need is exactly the same as you and I. I cannot take this lady to her former home but I can strive to give her a feeling of home through my service. In the end, I think we are the same, old and young alike.

That's enough for me today. I am going home.

1.2 Reflective practice on **"There's no place like home!" (Dorothy, Wizard of Oz). What does home mean to you?**

Key themes in this article

The meaning of home as security, comfort especially when afraid. Avoiding judgement. Seeing the person – good practice in dementia care.

What does this article mean to you?

What can / would you apply from this learning to your practice?

Other notes

1.3 Staff engagement / are we missing something?

I have noticed there is now a much greater focus on staff engagement, it seems to have become the elusive "holy grail" of management. The idea being that if staff were more engaged, the company could be more successful, with higher levels of productivity and staff retention. Sounds great but is it really achievable? The millionaire dollar question is how do we get our staff to REALLY engage with the business? I think this focus is a healthy thing. I have been lucky enough to work for several values based businesses that do get this right – however, in my experience this has proved to be the exception rather than the norm. In my view, I think there is a part missing when talking about staff engagement. I hope this article contributes to the debate. As usual it is based on experience, so with that disclaimer, lets proceed;

Firstly, considering how to get staff engaged – there has been much work done on this, needless to say, I would summarize this as focusing on a more humane, inclusive, responsive management model / style (think Virgin or various tech companies - open holiday entitlements and variable working hours at one end). I see this as building bridges of respect, understanding, agreeing expectations, treating staff like peers, sharing a mission. It is moving away from a strictly command and control, ego based style. There are some great recognition programmes which help foster these qualities but like a husband who buys a nice present for his wife one day and then shouts and screams the next day, engagement is not a one off gesture, it must be supported by other behaviours! It needs to be CONSISTENT and CONGRUENT. (I should know, some years ago I tried the chocolates without the follow through, the increased "engagement" was rather short lived!)

Secondly, rather than ask how do we engage or retain staff engagement, possibly we need to ask another question - what are we doing that the staff are habitually not engaged or disengaging. I take a view that many staff WOULD naturally be engaged but can be switched off by authoritarian management practices or line management practices, where the well-being of the staff is not considered adequately. In response, the team pull back. I have seen this happen SO many times. I like the metaphor of Stephen Covey about the emotional bank account – is performance / effort rewarded through the culture? In various places I have worked, the staff wonder, is it really worth going the extra mile for the business? In many cases, this where staff engagement is lost or more sadly, never gained.

Could it really as simple as this? Let's look at a quote from the UK Billionaire Sir Richard Branson about the importance of a positive, engaging culture at work;

"Colleagues should take care of each other, have fun, celebrate success, learn by failure, look for reasons to praise rather than criticise, communicate freely and respect each other. "

Lastly then, I put it to you that as a leader, whether your motivation is congruence to your company values or you simply adopt these values as enlightened commercial interest, it matters little. In my view, self-awareness and emotional intelligence are key attributes needed to make a success of this new paradigm. If in doubt, ask your peers to evaluate you honestly and listen, then adjust. There are "360 degree appraisals" which can help with this. Google this if unfamiliar. Please also see start with my article on personality type with teams - https://www.linkedin.com/pulse/how-i-developed-my-leadership-team-price-pizza-liam-palmer?trk=mp-author-card

In conclusion, let's not waste our precious human capital in the workplace through practicing or allowing behaviours in our workplace which disengage our staff and ultimately hurt the organisation. Enough talking, let's do this!

1.3 Reflective practice on **Staff engagement / are we missing something?**

Key themes in this article

Accountability, positive culture, congruence.

What does this article mean to you?

What can / would you apply from this learning to your practice?

Other notes

1.4 Got problem staff? What they need is a good..?

A good talking to? Really? A challenge with a difficult staff member has made me reconsider this. Certainly in times past, I may have framed some problems as due to "problem staff" based on them exhibiting moody, difficult, bad attitude behaviours. Now, I am not so sure whether this holds true. Let me explain;

This young lady would continually contradict me in the morning meeting – seeming to score points and taking time to resist the direction I was laying down. It was difficult, I noted and thought, I wonder why she is doing that? It happened a few more times. I didn't put her in her place – not really my style but would move things on. Other team members winced. Yes, it was uncomfortable, yes I am the Home Manager, and yes I need to take action but what action?

I decided to frame our chat to outline where I wanted to take the home – co-incidentally she had missed various other meetings I had given – she "was out of the loop." We sat down and this individual outlined how they operate. She shared her philosophy about work, management and tales where they felt intimidated or uncomfortable by former bosses.

Notwithstanding some unusual views, I found her to be decent and kind and true to herself. I simply said that I generally agreed and had a similar style. At the end, she said, "this has been insightful." I spoke for around 3 mins of the 1 hour. After this meeting, she was now supportive in those morning meetings, surprisingly the problematic behaviours stopped. I didn't really need to say anything but she had a need to be listened to.

In case this sounds like I am a wise sage, I am not. 10 years ago I would have talked and pressed my point. I am not wiser, simply OLDER! A lot of the time, it is really challenging to make this time, as managers we don't have it, and yet if the team member doesn't perform, how much time does it take to manage these behaviours? How much time is spent talking about them, getting advice, writing things up I wonder?

In the busyness of my day, I am going to try and keep my eyes and heart open to give that emotional support where it is really needed. I will choose to make that time. In the end I think everyone has a right to be heard and to be listened to.

1.4 Reflective practice on **Got problem staff? What they need is a good..?**

Key themes in this article

The power ad challenge of deep listening. The gift of affirmation. Focussing on our similarities rather than our differences. Give your staff unconditional positive regard (love) and accept them as they are.

What does this article mean to you?

What can / would you apply from this learning to your practice?

Other notes

1.5 Developing your team – Part 1 –fundamentals

Thank you for clicking this article - this is a real story of a real team, where we achieved a significant improvement accessing a management tool for the price of a meal for one. I have found this model is still relatively unknown, so let's start at the beginning.

For our purposes, our story starts with 2 U.S. citizens - Isabel Myers and her mother Katherine Cook Briggs. They both had a deep interest in the work of Carl Jung, the famed Swiss psychotherapist. During the second world war, when the men were sent away, women moved into industry. This mother and daughter team thought that a tool would help determine which role the new starters were best suited for. There was nothing available at the time and eventually it became their passion and life's work to produce this tool. Eventually, this led to the Myers Briggs Type Indicator (MBTI) tool that is still used today. For those who are new to this, or would enjoy a refresher on the basics, please see below;

* "The questionnaire is to help people realise their "best fit type". the personality type that will help them succeed most in life. The three original pairs of preferences in Jung's typology
are extraversion and intraversion, sensingand intuition and thinking and feeling. After studying them, Briggs Myers added a fourth
pair, judging and perceiving.

"Extraversion or Introversion: refers to where and how one directs his or her attention and energy — on people and things in the outer world, or alone in the inner world

Sensing or Intuition: refers to how one prefers to deal with information — by focusing on the basic information, or by interpreting and adding meaning

Thinking or Feeling: refers to decision making — objectively, using logic and consistency, or subjectively, considering other people and special circumstances

Judging or Perceiving: refers to how one interacts with the outer world — with a preference towards getting things decided, or for staying open to new information and options."

* MBTI Personality test / quoted from Wikipedia

After 30 years of research, we have a strong foundation of research to support the usefulness of the Myers Briggs Type Indicator (MBTI) tool and a new industry was born – typology within psychology.

Information on this tool can be found from their book "Gifts differing" and there are also online tests available to enable people to discover their profile / gifts. I am suggesting that 80% of the benefit of using this tool can be realised by reading this book and simply all your leadership team completing an online MBTI Inventory – though make sure it's the same one! In adopting this simplistic view, I know there will be those who may criticise this approach – to which I reply the following;

To the experts that say it is far more complex, I agree, I have just read a few books and make no claims except that in my experience being introduced to the model can be very enlightening for any team member. It can them to help them to understand and accept themselves and in turn respect their differences with colleagues too.

To the critics who say that this is an overly simplistic model and cannot possibly capture the complexity and nuances of the human personality – I agree, however, if we say that it simply helps people understand key differences of perception between themselves and others, herein for me, is the key to its value. Crucially, it also gives us a language to talk about it.

The original purpose of these pioneers was to help people identify their gifts – hence the title "Gifts differing" title quoted from Ephesians in the Good book. I think like Chinese whispers this has become distorted to become a process of categorizing a person. For me this misses the mark entirely.

We completed these tests for my team leaders and key support staff with some fascinating results. I hope that if you are not familiar with this work, it will spark an interest for you. I will share our findings in the next article. In the mean-time feel free to share your views about the use of this tool.

I hesitated to publish this first part of the article until today, one of my leadership team told me that the tipping point for her overcoming communications issues with staff was when she discovered her personality profile! Apparently, it made that much of a difference!

I dedicate this article to a former mentor Paul Brooks (Unipart / BIS / CILT). He introduced me to this model which later enabled me to embark on a major career transition – I appreciate the input - thank you!

1.5 Reflective practice on **Developing your team – Part 1 – underpinning theory**

Key themes in this article

That people's differences according to Myers Briggs are "gifts" to be developed and shared. Personal awareness. Self-knowledge. Making this info accessible at a negligible cost (consultants / trainers are a bonus but not necessary to get some benefits.)

What does this article mean to you?

What can / would you apply from this learning to your practice?

Other notes

1.6 Developing your team – Part 2 – in practice

Thank you for reading this article - it is the follow on from my previous one "Developing your team – Part 1 – fundamentals, where I outlined the advantages of using a personality profile model with your team. This can be accessed through free on-line tests and buying the book by the authors – for a very modest cost.

In this article, I want to talk about what we found when 7 key staff in my former care home took the Myers Briggs test and what that means to running a home and whether these findings could help with recruitment / succession planning.

Since the Myers Briggs model is a self-assessment with either / or questions, the following are generalisations based on observed differences in working with these individuals for just under a year. With that in mind, this is what I found;

Considering those with a T (thinking) preference as opposed to a F (feeling) preference

2 key staff - with people management responsibilities - both highly capable and respected had a "T" for thinking preference rather than "F" feeling preference in processing information. Everyone else (another 5) tested had an F preference. Co-incidentally both these staff struggled to influence their team. One quote was " I tell them what to do, I just don't understand why they don't do it". And another, " I just don't know what to do. I have told them; they just don't listen." Knowing them well, the context was that these individuals had less buy in from their colleagues and were perceived as less influential. They both did not possess the emotional calibration and sensitivity that many of their peers had but did benefit from coaching. Both were particularly strong in matters of governance and managing quality.

Considering those with an N (intuitive) preference as opposed to the S (senses) preference

Those staff with an intuitive preference or leaning were a minority and tended to think at multiple levels and conceptualise problems from different angles. The strongest ones were skilled problem solvers. The feedback was sometimes deep and insightful. Those with a sensing preference tended to have a more uniform, single dimensional approach.

Implications for managing carers

My key point here is that many carers (based on my observations) will have a "F" or feeling preference. In that sense they will instinctively prefer to be managed by someone who can relate to them in the same language (this can be learned).

Conclusions

Some staff profiles are more common / rarer than others - this was shown by Myers Briggs initial research. Judging by my research there seemed to be more people with a strong feeling preference (F) in this care home. In this work, there is a distinct need to provide compassionate care so those with that awareness seem to working in the right place!

Whilst every distinct profile will bring certain benefits however, what is most important in my view is a healthy mixture of different characters - a diverse culture which accepts the varying strengths all bring. This can be achieved through the leaders of the home being self-aware so they can understand themselves better and the value that differences bring. Thank goodness we don't need to be some sort of idealistic "perfect"!

Every combination of preferences has distinct leanings and strengths. Let's understand that and work together to create an inclusive and supportive work environment for all.

1.6 Reflective practice on Developing your team – Part 2 – in practice

Key themes in this article

Thinking / feeling preference- over representation of "feeling" bias people in care and the impact of this, in terms of their management. Self-knowledge, self- acceptance and self-love leads to harmony with others.

What does this article mean to you?

What can / would you apply from this learning to your practice?

Other notes

Part 2 – Masterclass in Home Leadership

Part 2 – Masterclass in Home Leadership - overview

In this Masterclass in Home Leadership, I look at some complex problems and established "challenges" within the care sector and take a contrary view to challenge some existing assumptions and paradigms.

Firstly, I start with acknowledging that being a home manager can be volatile if the operator does not have a supportive culture – I explain why this is bad for care.

Next, we look at the traditional argument that only nurses should run care homes – who leads best?

Next, we look at the biggest challenge in care – agency usage and how to move forward. There is so much misinformation in this area.

Lastly, we pull much of the material and learning together, to outline an approach that works regarding taking charge of a challenged home.

Part 2- Masterclass in Home Leadership -   Pg

2.1 High levels of Care Home Manager attrition   37

2.2 Care Home Manager – who leads best?   43

2.3 Facing the "agency problems" in UK Care Homes   47

2.4 Moving forward with the "agency problem"   51

2.5 How to take charge of a challenged home   55

2.1 High levels of Care Home Manager attrition are hurting the UK care home industry. This is why.

As usual, please excuse the generalisations taken to keep this article brief. Thanks to those linked-in contacts that shared their stories which inspired this article. Before getting into this, we need to establish some reference points;

a) UK Care Home Context

Firstly, I want to consider the UK care home context – that our model has evolved from a hospital ward, where patients were kept in rows and kept alive through basic nursing provision. From there, the model has evolved to provide single rooms, activities, higher standards and a need for extensive documentation to evidence good care. In many care providers there has been a cultural shift to a more individual and person centred model – all these developments are welcome. The CQC has moved from inspector to more recently champion of high standards of care management leadership – "is the home well lead, safe, effective, responsive, caring" – ask the CQC guidelines. My sense is that the industry is in catch up and that our IT systems, support systems, career development ladders all need to evolve to meet this higher requirement and to be able to sustain it.

b) Unexpected consequence of home manager accountability

Like most in the industry, I welcome greater accountability and transparency and the regulators stance on this, though I would make the point that the ecosystem of the wider care home environment needs to enable the home manager to meet these high requirements. With most care businesses making extensive use of paper to record key information, there is no systemised way of managing much information, inevitably this introduces an element of risk. Also with a mix of corporate, hybrid and independent players in the sector, IT systems have evolved but not in a uniform way. Many care businesses have multiple IT systems for different functions which don't communicate with each other. This makes the task of home manager more complex than it needs to be. Herein is a temporary pressure point – whilst home managers are accountable for all that happens in their homes, in many cases their supporting systems are somewhat under-developed. This leads to a new pressure point;

c) Home Manager attrition / the problem with that

By most estimates, Home Manager attrition is running at 25- 50% across the UK care home industry. We are building more units than ever and this will continue with a sharp upturn over the next 20 years, yet home manager attrition is unusually high. I can't definitively prove the following connection; however it is possible that this partly relates to the greater expectations of the CQC, tied in with personal accountability, with an operating environment that is in catch-up.

These high levels of home manager attrition are contrary to the needs of the residents in our homes;

d) The need for those in our care

In many of the best homes I have visited, I noticed some common denominators – often key staff posts (deputy / unit manager / nurse / administrator) have been in post for 3, 5, 10 years or more. Often long serving carers, who know all the families and residents help the home feel like an extended family. This leads to my main point, that our residents at the end of their lives need stability and that stability partly comes from the continuity of the home manager; we need to reduce the home manager attrition WHILST driving up standards.

e) Impact of home manager attrition on staff and compliance

This effects the residents and crucially the residual staff team – in some homes, no-one takes the home manager seriously because they change every 6 months! This is not good for continuity of care. As the leadership changes, the whole staff team goes back to a time of building and getting established – it causes staff to feel anxious. If it happens too often it can lead staff to fully disengage, to stop trusting the company or "management". In my experience, herein lies the seeds of dysfunctional homes, with long term compliance issues -the team are unstable and there is no core residual knowledge of good practices and mature relationships with associated professionals and families. In my view, a care home does not operate in isolation but is rather a part of a complex healthcare system and a myriad of supporting professionals and the individuals and families involved in the care, it is a physical meeting point for care provision.

f) What is the true scope of the Care Home Manager role?

Herein is the crux of the matter. As a job, in most homes, it will be to be compliant with the regulators, to use the company policies as appropriate, and follow the lead of the recruiting manager. These are all a given, however, for those who have run a home, it quickly becomes apparent that the role is more than this;

The home manager is the trusted individual for those who make a decision to put their loved one in care. When that son or daughter looks the home manager in the eye, they are trusting the home manager with their mum or dad, if the home manager keeps changing, it is unnerving and does not represent the company or industry in a positive light.

The home manager is also the chief story-teller of the home, they hold the history, the context, the reputation of the home and represent it to the council, regulators, healthcare professionals, families, community at large. They act as an ambassador for care, the brand of the organisation and of the local home. Lives come into the home and at the very end we see out those final days with the family - we hold hands with those that pass as they slip away. We've shared that journey with the family, touched humanity for a moment, it's a shared knowing that our life is also finite. It matters. Community and continuity matter in this context.

It is for these additional responsibilities that the high attrition upsets the care community they serve. The industry is going through a period of change, like a storm, the home managers are bravely facing it and following the steer of the regulator and employer. There are some great examples of enlightened care operators successfully grappling with these contradictory pressures of a need for continuity, a need for a raising of standards and the challenge of high levels of attrition for care home managers. They understand the value and importance of the home managers. It can be done.

Finally, then, let's try and keep community and stabilise this crucial position in the provision of care. Let's do it for those we serve and for the courageous home managers doing a difficult job, often with good cheer. Let's do all we can to raise standards and where possible reduce home manager attrition through up-skilling, developing more robust information and home management structures to enable them to lead with confidence and skill.

Dedicated to all the skilful Care Home Managers throughout the sector. Thanks for all you do.

2.1 Reflective practice on **High levels of Care Home Manager attrition are hurting the UK care home industry. This is why**

Key themes in this article

Cause and effect, balancing home manager accountability within the context, systems, support structures within which they work. Questioning whether managing standards through frequently moving on home managers is an effective strategy / and considering the impact on residents and teams when they are moved. Are there any other approaches which could be more effective?

What does this article mean to you?

What can / would you apply from this learning to your practice?

Other notes

2.2 Care Home Manager - who leads best- Clinical Manager or General Manager professional?

Whilst this is a very "tongue in cheek" question, in my experience this question is part of a genuine ongoing debate in UK care home leadership, where residents with nursing needs are involved. Chiefly, who leads best and in a time of increased rigour with the new regulator's framework (CQC), who has the most complete skills to get to a CQC rating of "good" or beyond? I write as a generalist who has been challenged by some former clinical colleagues claiming that only a nurse / clinical manager can "really" do it. Clearly there does need to be strong clinical leadership but is there always an advantage in that person also being the home manager? I explore below;

I greatly respect my nurse colleagues for the level of responsibility and skill they have, however, in my view, the skill of nursing is a profession in its own right, as is a Head Chef or a qualified Facility Management professional. Their jobs are organised with documentation, records, reporting protocols for legal and corporate governance and (in my experience) usually robust recruitment tools in place to ensure duties and responsibilities are clearly understood. The Home Manager has oversight of reporting, standards, audits and takes appropriate action as needed and leads by example, listening and supporting.

For my part, I have been determined to show that the distinction between the 2 disciplines is overstated. For example, no one would say that a clinical manager can't learn the theories of management science and leadership, in the same way, there is no reason why a professional and skilled general manager cannot learn the fundamentals of the clinician. In my own small way, I have tested this. After 18 months, I have finished my Diploma in Clinical Science with a Higher Merit. I am very grateful for the support of the BSY Group tutor and recommend this to my non-clinician fellow managers. Was it challenging? Yes! Understanding "peak flow, urticaria, oncogenic theory and target diastolic blood pressure" was as a foreign language to me! However, I discovered that the fundamentals are not so hard to grasp as there is a sense and structure to this body of knowledge. In fact, fear was my greatest challenge over and beyond the technical complexity.

In conclusion, I think a better question is - how can we develop clinical home managers to strengthen their general management / leadership skills and how can we develop the clinical knowledge of generalist home managers? Whilst we consider this, I believe we need to respect the complementary strengths that each approach brings. In my view, there is no "perfect" care home manager, there is just you and me, learning, growing, doing our best every day and drawing on the teams around us. Inevitably we'll all always be stronger in some things than others and after all, running a home is a team effort. I am comfortable with that.

2.2 Reflective practice on "Care Home Manager - who leads best..Clinical Manager or General Manager professional?

Key themes in this article

Appreciating the differences. Teamwork. Importance of upskilling and personal and professional development.

What does this article mean to you?

What can / would you apply from this learning to your practice?

Other notes

2.3 Facing the "agency problem" in UK care homes

With the minimum wage rising, and a funding gap with the publicly funded beds, care home operators are under particularly acute financial pressure, one area that could help is a sustained reduction in the use of agency staff.

Having had some useful debate with many of you very experienced and skilled home managers, I thought it may be helpful to take a fresh look at this "problem" and see if we agree what that problem is. This list is not exhaustive but instead a start;

a) Is the problem - management comfort and over-use of agency which is putting a great strain on the care industry finances? (If so, the primary solution will be about the control of the ordering of agency - approval and sign off going to higher levels of management to control / dissuade its use.)

b) Is the problem a lack of recruitment leading to an over-reliance use on agency - either through a lack of contracted hours or possibly a lack of precision about recruiting into the right areas for example? If so, putting energy into recruitment in a targeted way should solve this.

c) Is the problem about the sustainability of the location - i.e. local competition (supermarkets etc.) with wages, or perhaps a lack of transport links for staff to get to the home?

d) Is the problem a lack of managerial understanding about finance? (If so, easily fixed by a skilled mentor to a receptive home manager.)

e) Is the problem caused / aggravated by excessive sickness levels? How about staff retention levels? How about holiday management - is it well controlled?

f) How about the budget - are there sufficient hours to run adequately or is it too tight, putting undue pressure on skilled staff?

g) Is this part of a wider issue of a growing economy (reduced labour pool to draw from)? If this is a continued trend, do the options for career advancement for the carers / nurses need to be looked at (with a nod to Terry Tucker - I know this was something you have done some great work on.)

h) If the agency usage is primarily nursing - does this relate to the national shortage? Or are their wider issues in the home causing nurses not to stay? What strategies are the organisation using to address this? Are they working? Does the organisation have a culture where this level of honest communication / integrated problem solving can take place?

i) If the agency usage is primarily carers - are the wages competitive with other care homes in the area?

I guess I am trying to make the point that in my view, often agency usage per se is not the primary issue but rather a symptom of something or several things not working optimally in a specific care home ecosystem / wider industry. I am convinced that understanding the inter-relatedness of these matters is crucial.

Addressing these issues requires confident leadership from the top, balancing the quality message with cost control. In my view, it requires team spirit to share information broadly and confident managers who listen and empower teams to come up with elegant, tailored, local solutions.

I have been fortunate to meet and work with some excellent senior managers in care over the last few years. I have seen some successful agency reduction models working allied with supportive leadership, balancing quality and safety and cost. It shows that it can be done. For me, it's a call to leadership. Game on!

2.3 Reflective practice on Facing the "agency problem" in UK care homes

Key themes in this article

Robust critical thinking, a balanced approach, cause and effect, accountability, courage to face difficult problems.

What does this article mean to you?

What can / would you apply from this learning to your practice?

Other notes

2.4 Moving forward with the "agency problem" in UK care homes. How do we reduce reliance on agency staff? What works?

This is a follow up to my last article - Facing up to the "agency problem". My key take away was that the "agency problem" was not the problem but rather its habitual use highlighted areas in the care ecosystem not working effectively. In my view, it is a call to radical problem solving and integrated leadership within social care.

Moving on then, what can we do to reduce reliance on agency staff? This is a broad area, so please forgive the generalisations and omissions as I attempt to answer this as concisely as possible;

Opportunities for avoiding reliance on nursing agency;

In the UK, there is a nursing shortage and it's acute in certain geographical areas however, let us not use that as an excuse to avoid the hard work required to keep attracting and retaining skilful nurses. Let's consider what we can do; we can present our home or company well, have an attractive package and role. We can offer a well-managed home with a supportive management culture and room for progression. We can make our home the employer of choice for nurses in our area. We can aim to have the best managed home in the area, with the best cared for residents - right?! I accept that we are limited in the pool of talent but surely this calls for greater flexibility and persistence to differentiate our workplace from our competitors. If all we do is improve retention - that can REALLY help reduce reliance on nursing agency. Let's review our assumptions, learn from others and action, action, action!

Opportunities for avoiding reliance on carer agency workers; For many this the greatest opportunity. Let's look at "what works."

I have been involved in reducing agency reliance across several homes and consulted with many. Where there is habitual use of carer agency, providing there are not more complex issues at play (see last article), the most common cause is insufficient recruitment. In my experience this is either due to;

i) A lack of focus or recruitment process resource so the home is below the curve - carers take 4 - 12 weeks to bring on board. Recruitment needs to start before they are needed in the rota. Timing is key. (work 2 - 3 months ahead and take some measured risks on predicted occupancy.)

ii) A company imposed limit on carer hours which doesn't have enough slack to allow for leavers and the inevitable variation of occupancy. Where the tolerance around hours is too lean, with little discretion, agency reliance is far more likely. Like a bell curve, if we recruit too near the average (contracted hours), we will have too many days that are an exception - (solved by allowing a greater variation on contracted hours to cover sickness and the natural variations found in running a care home.)

Other contributory factors are;

iii) Cultural acceptance - key staff involved in the rota, and covering shifts may have got used to calling the agency when a need arises, rather than putting more energy into local efforts to cover through the team. Also, the home can get attached to certain agency workers and keep booking them (thanks DB for the anecdote!). (solved by Home Manager addressing robustly).

iv) The sickness policy is not being consistently applied. (easily remedied)

v) There is a lack of co-ordination and planning regarding holidays. (easily remedied.)

vi) There is particularly poor staff retention. Staff don't want to stay - .(retention stats will tell a story as will the body language and staff engagement on the floor. Support visits should bring this to light.)

Conclusion - let's be relentless in challenging excuses, blame and rise to the challenge by skilfully reducing reliance on agency staff, where there is potential to do so. In the meantime, agency staff and their companies are an integral part of care delivery - let 's work with them effectively, treat their staff well and appreciate the contribution they make to our services and those in our care.

2.4 Reflective practice on **Moving forward with the "agency problem" in UK care homes. How do we reduce reliance on agency staff? What works?**

Key themes in this article

Focus on taking action that will help. Understand what are the primary drivers are and where possible, take charge.

What does this article mean to you?

What can / would you apply from this learning to your practice?

Other notes

2.5 How to take charge of a challenged mid – large care home. What works?

I was emboldened to write this after speaking with other peers from different businesses - it turned out they had had used a similar solution with comparable results. As always, please excuse the generalisations needed to keep the article brief. To be clear, this is simply an outline of one effective approach.

Firstly, I need to define some of the problems and how to interpret those problems;

Why do care homes get out of control?

The reasons for this are complex – I have talked to many of you about this – here is a selection of common causes you mentioned;

It can simply be a couple of staff leave in quick succession – leading to a flurry of leavers. Then agency use goes up, morale can suffer and care quality can be affected. Since it often takes 6 – 8 weeks to recruit key staff and that leavers often only give a months' notice or less, this is common. (Maybe the industry should consider giving a 2-month notice for particular positions? Food for thought

It can be ineffective leadership by a head of department, or the home manager or serious misconduct by a couple of staff.

It can be a manager with a set of skills not well suited to the needs in that particular home.

It can be a dropping of standards in one or more areas left unchallenged or staff displaying problematic behaviours that have not been successfully addressed – impacting morale and team performance.

As mentioned in the last article on care home manager attrition – a revolving door approach for managers can, over time destabilise a staff team and by implication, the home.

It can be the effect of having the wrong staff in post.

It can be support staff primarily focussing on finding fault, rather than on building competence and confidence, (not supporting.)

It can be the impact of a CQC inspection which lacks objectivity and needs to be challenged.

What is the connection between these items?

I would make 3 observations – firstly that a care home is an integrated operation – all parts are interdependent – a weakness in one area, will affect other areas and it can happen very quickly.

Secondly, in light of the above point, there may be no one party responsible for difficulties – maybe it is simply a dynamic that has been created in the home. We need to be careful about having a quick swoop in and identifying the problem before executing the solution.

Thirdly, the home is only as strong as its reputation. If people start finding fault, a sense of negativity and fear can consume the home. I am convinced that we need to emphasise operating in good faith, as a healthy team and trust each other. We need to strike a balance between positively supporting and promoting a home with dealing robustly with ineffective care and challenging poor practices.

The big picture

When you look at the list of reasons given for a home getting unstuck, it can be impossible to work out which of these overlapping points is at play, which is the primary cause? For me, this is why we need skilled managers and leaders in the sector. However, stepping away from this, my question is - what is it about care home management structures (particularly in mid to large homes) that makes this problem so common?

Key weakness in care home structures

Whilst the roles in a care home are usually well defined, in many cases, there is an under-developed (compared to industry) management structure. Secondly, communication and problem solving skills are often lacking. In my view, at the heart of this is a lack of sound management practice. Likely this is in part from the evolution of care from being a medical unit, part of a hospital and also because the nurses running many homes have received little management training. This can be remedied by more training, study and from the cross-fertilisation of skills from other management professionals moving into care.

How does this work itself out in care / why does it impact homes getting out of control?

Where the deputy or home manager, work in a personal way (have their favourites / punish or reward those go their way) and wraps all decision making around them to bolster their position – it exposes the home to a risk of being destabilised with a number of ills;

Risk of political culture/ low morale

By working in this way, it sets a poor example to staff around – since it is not a meritocracy, politics are rife rather than a focus on good care and teamwork.

Waste of talent

By under-utilising nurses, carers, seniors, unit managers, we dis-empower them. We are wasting a great deal of talent.

Low productivity / risk

By doing this, we are usually behind in key tasks because these key people are overworked, have made themselves near "indispensable" to the operating of the home.

What can we do to address this?

Step 1 - Have a manager with empowerment, coaching and strategic management skills to assist.

Step 2 – look to develop a structure of mini-leaders under the deputy / home manager which is well defined and effectively delegates certain tasks to each of these, whilst retaining accountability with the home manager. In my experience, this is most effectively done by the following;

Step 3 – redefine job descriptions so that these roles are aligned, agreed with staff, rewarded fairly, supernumerary hours needed are all signed off and agreed. Launch in a way that the whole home supports the new positions. Conduct a transparent interview process so that a sense of fairness prevails.

Step 4 – develop this group as a cohesive team, teach them problem solving, communication skills, and coaching skills with tools to make sure they do report up necessary information so that overall control is retained by the home manager.

In conclusion - this works simply because it utilises talent, cost effectively leverages the un-used talent in the home and liberates the home manager to oversee, direct, lead, troubleshoot rather than working in a more traditional, administration focussed approach to the role.

2.5 Reflective practice on **How to take charge of a challenged mid – large care home. What works?**

Key themes in this article

Team dynamics. The impact of individual / group behaviours. Skills lacking. Using structure / empowerment to improve performance.

What does this article mean to you?

What can / would you apply from this learning to your practice?

Other notes

Part 3 – Masterclass in Leadership Qualities

Part 3 – Masterclass in Leadership Qualities – overview

True empathy as distinct from compassion, kindness or sympathy is a very effective quality in human relations, especially useful in care. In the first article about "having a bad day..I look at some of our assumptions and judgements and how they can block connection.

Next, I look at the qualities of gratitude and appreciation. Many of us, (myself included) can be so focussed on what's ahead, we can miss the beauty right in front of us.

Next I use a story about a career change to explain the importance of flexibility and versatility to meaningful goal achievement.

Next, I look at the quality of persistence and the surprising outcomes of not being moved by circumstances.

Lastly, I look at inspiration - most effective leaders are inspired in some way and this was an example of great love leaving a legacy.

Part 3 – Masterclass in Leadership Qualities   Pg

3.1 Empathy   Having a bad day   67

3.2 Gratitude   What could be more beautiful?   71

3.3 Flexibility How I made a change   75

3.4 Persistence When all seems lost   79

3.5 Inspiration What inspires you?   83

3.1 Empathy –

Having a "bad" day / an unexpected gift from a stranger in Birmingham City Centre

So here I was, let me just front this, I was having a "bad" day - mercifully it doesn't happen to me that often but today, this was it. The forces of chaos on several levels had got to me. I was fed up with my lot. It would pass, yet at that point, it was bearing heavy on me. I couldn't see a solution.

I was in Birmingham City Centre, as I walked to my car, I saw a young guy sleeping under a concrete stairwell, a filthy area and his older friend, like a father hanging around anxiously, both of European descent. I saw them tentatively, had a sense whether they were on drugs / alcohol. Were they safe I wondered? I am used to people asking for money or whatever and take a view based on each person I meet. For me, it's a fine line between getting hardened and not being a soft touch. I try to stay aware.

This gentleman wanted to show me his stuff, some basic toiletries very carefully put in a clean bag. It was a strange juxtaposition of chaos and order and he was so particular about maintaining this order in this little bag. The squalor of his living arrangements and the chaos of actually living on the street were hard to fathom. He was wanting to show me his life. I tried to empathise for a minute, he was quite lucid but broken, ashamed and slightly confused. I considered how it would be. It was heart breaking. I saw a couple of small bottles of alcohol but he wasn't under the influence. I quizzed him about it. I worried that I was giving him money to buy alcohol. In doing so, I felt bad. It felt like I was trying to get him to justify needing help. I was embarrassed of myself. He could have been my father.

I searched in my pocket, found a £10 note and gave it to him. He paused for about 5 seconds and then started crying. A grown man just started crying like that. I was pained. He was a man of dignity and self-respect, not knowing what to do, living on apples by the looks of it. My problems didn't go away that day but that gentleman gave me a reality check. I wasn't living under a concrete stairwell; I wasn't living on a diet of apples in a strange land, showing a stranger all he had in the world. I felt he was trying to get a connection and by talking to me, trying to get a sense of order in the chaos of his life right there.

He pointed at a carefully folded bit of paper with his name on and with a little broken English, explained next week, once he got to an embassy, he would be ok. He just needed to get through till then, He said he would split the money with his friend. He wanted me to know that.

Oh my friend, I did judge you for a moment, I am sorry. You are better than I and the gift you gave me was far greater than which I gave you. Thank you.

3.1 Reflective practice on **Having a "bad" day / an unexpected gift from a stranger in Birmingham City Centre.**

Key themes in this article

Empathy, other centeredness, avoiding judgements. How a giving heart often brings its own unexpected reward

What does this article mean to you?

What can / would you apply from this learning to your practice?

Other notes

3.2 Gratitude

What could be more beautiful? A time of reflection.

The inspiration for this brief share was a gentleman sharing on a video about his love for his children. In September 2015, Abdullah Kurdi lost his wife and 2 children whilst making his way to Europe as a refugee. The photo of his little boy on a beach made headlines all around the world. He was interviewed and the reporter asked him what were your children like? He said "my kids were amazing. They woke me every day to play with me. What could be more beautiful than that?"

Predictably it's a time of reflection – this space is crowded with mantras of saying "thank you", daily gratitude's, mindfulness, resolutions and plans - good things in and of themselves but I wonder whether we can still miss what is in front of us – our everyday "problems and challenges." Here I am talking about the mid-range everyday stuff of life- from work, home, partner, kids, health, money – all of which can weigh heavy at times.

I don't know about you but I have spent a lot of time looking back, lots of time forward, the challenge for me is to spend more time in today. I want to ask you to look at your life afresh, look at your "problems and challenges" and see whether there is beauty there. Could some of the wonder have got lost with the busyness and pressures in life? *NLP talks about how we associate emotions with different things, for some maybe there's no longer a feeling of joy. Let's consider some common "problems."

Are you experiencing any of the following?

Problems or dissatisfaction with your home – you have a home – hopefully warm, secure. Can that feel good?

Problems with your partner – you have a partner, been loved, taken seriously. Have a companion. Can that feel good?

Problems with your kids? You have kids one way or the other and you are a parent. How good is that?

Problems with your health? You are alive, have lived, hopefully had some good times to date with more to come. Can that feel good?

Problems with finances? Have you enjoyed the use of money in your life so far – cars, holidays, new clothes, homes, meals, decent food? Can that feel good?

I do not say that significant problems are not serious - they require our best attention and personally I don't subscribe to the notion that suffering is merely relative. For me, each person's suffering is personal to them and to be taken seriously with compassion, empathy, support. Every person's resources and levels of strength are different. We need to help each other where we can. I simply say that sometimes there is beauty behind your "problems", if you look a little closer.

3.2 Reflective practice on **What could be more beautiful? A time of reflection.**

Key themes in this article

The importance of gratitude, the pre-eminence of family, living in the now, family bonds.

What does this article mean to you?

What can / would you apply from this learning to your practice?

Other notes

3.3 Flexibility

How do you make a mid-life career change? I made mine at 39. Here is what I learnt;

After many good years in operations management, I came to a point where my heart just wasn't in it anymore. Deep within, I had shifted, I felt different, yet in many ways I was at the top of my own game, with lots of experience, attractive job offers, yet I wanted out, yet out to what? How do you know what to get out to?

Winding forward, I did make that transition from logistics to managing 10 departments in a wonderful private hospital in the Thames Valley. For those of you considering a significant career transition, I would love to share a formula that you could use but instead I will give you my experience and feel free to take your own meaning from it. I hope that is useful.

I had thought about moving into private healthcare, though it was undefined in my mind. It was more a direction than a plan. This changed when I went on a guided walk in central London. A nurse met me on the walk and told me about an excellent private hospital group. I got intrigued. Next, a middle management opening came up a commutable location for the same group. I gave the application ALL I could. I put in 14 hours - I precisely mapped across every experience and competence requirement. In my view, it was objectively "perfect". Excitedly I received my letter from them the next day, surely confirming my interview date? I felt like Jim Carrey in the "Yes Man" movie - here was a door opening by providence! Actually, not for long! They declined my application. It was a dead-end, yet I felt so strongly about the fit, I decided to ask for feedback. The gentleman in question was very busy running 2 hospitals. I kept calling him and eventually we talked. It was delicate. I explained it was me who had failed to clearly articulate the fit. He warmed slightly on the call, we did connect. He conceded that if our candidates don't measure up, we will invite you for interview. He offered me crumbs. I was hungry and not proud. I WANTED to move across. Crumbs are a start!

Later, I did get the call and I met this gentleman at interview. There was a fit. Half an later, I had a job offer. This was from the same guy who wrote a letter to me saying "sorry, you have not been successful". My career in private healthcare, (whatever that was) had started! I worked with some great people and will always be grateful to that business for giving me a chance.

What did I learn - firstly that my instinct was right, my skills WERE relevant and transferable. On balance, the transition worked well. Secondly, the career transition was scary. Without any sponsors in management, I was on my own. It forced me to dig very deep into my own resources and self-confidence. In conclusion, I guess if you want something enough, you make it happen. That attitude abides with me now. I read somewhere that "hope is not a strategy". I agree. I learnt that if I want it enough, MOVE OUT OF THE WAY, I am going to MAKE it happen!

3.3 Reflective practice on **How do you make a mid-life career change? I made mine aged 39. Here is what I learnt;**

Key themes in this article

Perseverance. Drive. Being indefatigable. Refusing to accept "no.". Personal confidence, accurate inventory of transferable skills. Stepping up.

What does this article mean to you?

What can / would you apply from this learning to your practice?

Other notes

3.4 Persistence

Bouncing back from redundancy / how I used linked-in to get a better position

So for those of who caught my last post, there I was in my new career in a private hospital. I had worked hard- many 7 day weeks to deepen my knowledge and create something special there. I'd improved customer service, teams were developed, absence was reduced, individuals coached, developed and promoted. IT systems implemented, physical spaces developed with skill. I was feeling confident until I got that call. "Due to funding changes...we can no longer...we want to keep our best people but.".. They were a professional outfit, supportive, decent even but.. I had a month.

When this happened to a predecessor, she broke down crying, she became critical of the business and after a couple of days didn't work her leave. That's not my way. Of course, I was shocked but for me professionalism is key. I didn't let on to colleagues until a couple of days before my month was up. I had invested myself in this work and my team. I wasn't going to change who I was due to my role coming to an end. Initially I struggled to redefine my career goals, I felt a bit lost. Within a couple of weeks, I got clear; my destination was now the sector, the values of the business, the exact make-up of the role and employer were now flexible. With this brief, I got onto google, searching for "General Manager Healthcare". This led me to create a deliberate linked-in strategy;

As I was moving from private hospital to elderly care, I felt I needed to redefine myself. I set my linked-in tagline for the role I wanted rather than what I was doing. I laid out my stall - a description of my story, why I was moving from hospital to care. Next I started deliberately connecting with my target peers - care home managers and senior support staff in the right organisations. I was transparent about why I wanted to connect - everyone who questioned my reason for connection, did later accept the connection. Then something happened, the MAGIC started at 800 connections.

Let me explain before it appears this is a magic number. It is not. It relates to having added 700 industry specific connections in the area I wanted to move into and being a second degree connection with their contacts. It starts making you VISIBLE. It increases your chances of getting "lucky". That's when the phone started to ring. I met a remarkable recruiter (D - you know who you are) who told me about this fantastic company. After a very successful year with a quality competitor, I now work there.

"Luck Is What Happens When Preparation Meets Opportunity" Seneca

To close, in case I leave the impression that this was inevitable, that it was some kind of cosmic good luck, I can honestly say the opportunity came as challenge and constraint - it was for me to create the break I wanted. Luck / fate / the universe may have played a part (if so, thanks!) but it is not something I have learned to rely on. A respected doctor and colleague from that hospital said something quite profound to me when I left - she said in time, you will see this as a step that takes you to much GREATER things. I looked in her eye, she WAS being sincere. Within a year she was absolutely right. I am really grateful to that GP for her vision and belief in me. I am also grateful to my elderly care employers giving me a chance, an opportunity to work in this sector. I LOVE working with the elderly. You know who you are - Thank you.

3.4 Reflective practice on **Bouncing back from redundancy / how I used linked-in to get a better position.**

Key themes in this article - Initiative, flexibility, using new technology, lateral thinking,

What does this article mean to you?

What can / would you apply from this learning to your practice?

Other notes

3.5 Inspiration

What inspires you to do the work you do?

On a recent overseas trip, I was asked about my motivation for my work as a care home manager – it got me thinking; without hesitation it was my maternal grand-mother, Lillian McGeehan of Portsmouth. Why did this family member exert such an positive influence – still missed keenly 25 years on? Here's some thoughts;

Lillian lived 1910 – 1989. One of 10 brothers and sisters from Plymouth – many of which worked in the houses of gentry / or on a farm – a very different time. All the family somehow fitted in a 2 up, 2 down home and were by all accounts happy. She ran away with a young (Catholic) man (big deal as she was Church of England) called Jimmy McGeehan – a kind hearted but tough talking Glaswegian.

He moved his wife to Portsmouth for a better life – he was a skilled mechanic / engineer and later worked on the famous Concorde airplane. They had 2 lovely daughters – Heather (my mum) and Gloria. He was away a lot for work and liked a drink or two when he returned – as a result, home-life was not always harmonious (this is war / post war 1940's to 1950's) yet to my Gran, he was always her hero.

By the time I got to know my Gran well – she stayed with us for a few months and we would go to visit her a few times a year. She then lived alone on the 16th floor flat of a high rise block in Southsea, Portsmouth – I guess it was a council building – all I remember was the amazing view of the Guildhall, it felt like being on top of the world. It all seemed very grand and yet I guess it was humble too.

We would go with Gran to the seafront – to the pier with the amusements, peddleboats, fish and chips, go swimming, lovely happy times with my brothers. During my teenage times (was very tall, slim and moody! – no real change then, ok not quite so slim), we would go and see gran. She was so small; in her last years she was had shrunk from around 4'11 to 4'8'. So when I was 6' 3 at 14, when she opened the door she was staring at my waist – and slowly look up, with the biggest smile you ever saw – "my boys, my boys".

Apparently I was the spitting image of her late husband Jimmy (some genetic throwback I gather.)

One particular moment summed up this lady – when getting ready for our visit, she had spent the whole day carrying these relatively huge bags back full of all the food we liked – fish fingers, Neapolitan ice cream, crisps, coke, boxes of maltesers – good times! She was exhausted but just wanted us to have a great time with her, to look after us. We watched TV on a small black and white TV in those days next to an old piano full of black and white pictures of family.

Another time, she went to her purse, got literally all her pension money (maybe £60) and said "here you go my boys. Take it" My eldest brother and I were moved beyond words – I still choke up when mentioning it. We wouldn't take it. It was such a generous and selfless, near wreck-less act – I still reflect on that often. I think it was the sheer pleasure of seeing us and joy she had with us that still remains.

Maybe that's it – that sense of unconditional love. In counselling circles, they talk about unconditional positive regard – same sort of thing. I think I have expressed a few times, in my work as a psychotherapist and I hope in my work as a care home manager. It is something that I aspire to and yet fall short more often.

In memory of my tiny gran Lillian McGeehan – thank you, we still miss you.

3.5 Reflective practice on **What inspires you to do the work you do?**

Key themes in this article

The power of personal stories, family stories. Unconditional love. The legacy of a life well lived.

What does this article mean to you?

What can / would you apply from this learning to your practice?

Other notes

Part 4 – "revolving doors" and "managing the greatest risk"

Part 4 overview

In these 5 articles we have 2 sets of 2 – defining a problem and offering a solution and lastly revisiting my first article 2 years into care – will I still be able to say "Care Home Manager – best job in the world?!" Find out in the update in 4.5.

The first 2 articles 4.1 and 4.2 I talk about care home manager turnover (attrition). In September 2018, 2 years after I wrote this, the problem is becoming more pronounced. Several factors feed into this, many new homes are run by operators with unrealistic expectations around performance on compliance / occupancy in the first 2 years. This has a bearing*. I also have some reports of certain CQC inspectors applying the KLOE model in such an unyielding way that minor issues are being considered as major compliance issues. This can lead to a downgrade in a home's overall CQC rating. In many cases this can lead to reputational and financial damage to the home often without sufficient cause. This in turn can permanently affect the employment status of the home manager. Thankfully this is the exception rather than the norm but is still worth considering.

The next articles 4.3 and 4.4 I discuss "the greatest risk" and how to manage it. Every home manager I've spoken to agrees with this assessment – I hope you find it of interest! Feel free to e mail me – my contact details are on the last page if you want to share an anecdote.

*see Sara Livadeas excellent guide produced with Care England, "Opening a new care home" by Social Care Works ltd, www.socialworks.org.uk

Part 4 contents – "revolving doors" and "managing the greatest risk"

4.1 What is the cost…of having a "revolving door" for home managers? **PG 93**

4.2 With the "revolving door"..do you want to break the pattern? **PG 97**

4.3 Beware! The greatest risk in your Care Home/….facility today! **PG 103**

4.4 Managing the "greatest risk in your care home" today **PG 107**

4.5 ..Home Manager – ..best job in the world! Reflections 2 years on.**PG 111**

4.1 What is the cost to a Care / Nursing home of having a "revolving door" for home managers?

For those of who read my article on care home manager attrition, you will recall me saying that constantly changing home managers due to minor ills in a home is often not in the best interest of the service. It can be de-stabilising and counter-productive in the longer term. Where this happens several times in a row – we have to step back and ask ourselves some searching questions. Are our recruitment processes faulty? Is there some other dynamic at play? In my view, not attending to / or being aware of these other dynamics is what creates the "revolving door" for managers in a home.

Aside from the collateral damage to a manager's career that joins a service with systemic issues and leaves prematurely, the impact on resident's well-being and staff morale (all important issues in their own right); there is also a significant loss to the home as a commercial entity. I know giving care is not about money per se but they need to be well-funded to be self-sustaining and retain the support of investors. A financially healthy home, region, division, company is good for patient care as success leads to more investment and stability.

Let's have a quick look at the financial impact of a home without a stable, fully capable manager. The numbers are conservative industry averages. In my experience outside care, where service is not strong, sales will inevitably suffer.

When a home or care community is not "well led", occupancy will suffer and the homes finances will be affected;

Annual cost of a home without a stable, fully capable manager (40 beds)

Cost of recruitment fees x 2 managers + induction costs
£40k

Missing revenue target for a 40 bed (2 short of budget per month)   £90k

Missing annualised profit (EBITDA) target for a 40 bed   £45k

Extra recruitment / training days for higher attrition	£10k
Carer agency due to staff attrition	£15k
Lowest avge cost to a 40 bed home is £40k+£45k+£10k+£15k	**110k**

Annual cost of a home without a stable, fully capable manager (80 beds)

Cost of recruitment fees x 2 managers + induction costs	£40k
Missing revenue target for a 40 bed (4 short of budget per month)	180k
Missing annualised profit (EBITDA) target for an 80 bed	£90k
Extra recruitment / training days for higher attrition	£20k
Carer agency due to staff attrition	£25k
Lowest average cost to an 80 bed home is £40k+£90k+£20k+£25k	**175k**

These numbers ignore the extremes of homes with severe problems - the cost of a turnaround team and other internal specialists. Homes with severe agency problems (can be up to £100k per month, if a lack of carer AND nurses in a larger home.) If nurses are disgruntled, it can escalate to attrition. When a few leave, the burden of extra responsibility can lead to a complete clear out of contracted nurses. When you consider that covering a nurse vacancy through an agency costs twice as much, you can see how home problems can lead to costs spiralling out of control VERY quickly. This ignores homes with embargoes on new admissions.

There are other costs (my finance colleague JH tells me) which have a bearing;

"Reputation damage and if part of a group - group impact of reputation - the "Chinese whisper" effect. Cost controls in a home not being well managed , poor capital spending, lack of maintenance in a service leading to poor quality environment . Staff turnover with change of management leading to long term recruitment issues and shrinking pool of staff to recruit from. "

It is sobering isn't it? Where there is a constant churn of home managers in a particular home, we need to review how we are framing the "problems". Clearly just changing the manager is not working. We need a new paradigm and a different response that gets us better results.

4.1 Reflective practice on **What is the cost to a Care / Nursing home of having a "revolving door" for home managers?**

Key themes in this article

The financial value of loyalty and commitment over the mid to long term. Managing quality. Blame vs. problem solving. Owning issues. The financial benefit of keeping a sound manager vs. frequent changes of manager.

What does this article mean to you?

What can / would you apply from this learning to your practice?

Other notes

4.2 Does your Care / Nursing home have a "revolving door" for Home Managers? Do you want to break the pattern?

For those who read my previous article on care home manager attrition, you will recall that it is my belief that REGULARLY changing home managers in the SAME home due to minor ills is often not in the services interest. It can often be destabilising and counter-productive in the longer term. In the last article - we looked at the actual financial cost. In this article, we look at one way to break this pattern.

The UK regulator (CQC) guidelines are demanding a significant lift in quality and teamwork which can only be achieved through EFFECTIVE LEADERSHIP (CQC terms "well-led"). I am of the view that many home managers in our sector need to UPSKILL to meet these more robust standards of compliance.

This article is about a home that I was involved in - coaching a home manager and his team to break this pattern. We did break the pattern! Whilst I think much of this was due to the quality of this particular home manager, it may be helpful to review we learnt. My only reservation in sharing, is giving the possible impression of promoting my own work - that is not my intent, forgive me if it comes across that way. Rather, I wanted to show the approach required to deal with these underlying issues. If you're good with that, let's continue.

This was the brief I received;

A manager new to care, 5 months in post. He was sound but needed some support. The staff team were somewhat disengaged. I needed to go in as a support manager, sort the documentation, get the company protocols going and move on.

After digging much deeper, I discovered that;

The last 8 managers lasted between 3 months to just over a year - there had never been a stable home manager since it had opened 8 years ago. The last couple of deputies failed too – it strongly suggesting a cultural / systemic dynamic at play. This manager had received very little induction to care. I decided to tackle it from all angles, see if the pattern could be broken. I decided to take charge and go for the prize – a more stable home for the residents and those that work there.

Before I outline our approach, let's zoom to the end of the study and look at some of what we did achieve in 4 weeks with 3 x 1 day follow ups;

Positively and permanently resolved issues with under-performing Chef and administrator.

Positively and permanently resolved issues with under-performing carers (1 grievance, 1 departure, 1 passive aggressive response.) and 1 nurse

Conducted many whole home meetings - this established the "voice" of the home manager. We did them together, I gradually withdrew, he made it his own.

I held 19 individual staff supervisions and relayed all the information to the Home Manager with commitments given.

We finally integrated the nurses with the carers (it had been a "them and us" culture before. We created a team ethos.

We completely re-did the whole rota, reviewed clinical skill-mix after consulting with ALL staff. We listened, adapted, worked with the staff.

In 4 weeks we took an out of sector manager, with good knowledge of the company systems but lacking awareness of how to lead the home and coached him to become a strong, decisive, successful and respected home manager. He is a VERY strong leader-manager now.

We resolved 2 further grievances with no further grievances. (It was all running well..staff were happier!)

Staff attrition stopped. (it had been very high)

In case you wondered, no, it was not MAGIC! It was a systematic hunting for information about the cause of the disengagement and weaknesses in the home, checking this information from many perspectives and then executing well, demonstrating managerial competence and winning team members support and trust.

You see, it was the systemic issues in the home coupled with the skills gaps with the manager that could have led the revolving door to continue had we not taken a different approach. First of all, we needed to know what was REALLY happening in the home. To get that required demonstrating integrity, service and building trust.

The integrity was the first piece - that I would be a support to the manager, a coach (not spy!). I promised I would not undermine him. That took some time, I had to prove it to get his trust. Next was service - I served him, served the team, demonstrated by example. I constantly showed that the main thing is service and LEADING the home well. Trust came as these qualities were practiced consistently.

It was a tricky assignment to break this pattern - firstly because there was just 4 weeks, I needed to hit the home like a cyclone to get all the work done. Secondly, I needed to educate the manager. Be directive but gain his consent at all times - it was his home. Once the work was done and as his competence increased, I needed to withdraw and continually reinforce his autonomy.

At first, he did not understand why I was taking the approach I did, he looked at form and didn't perceive its significance. However, as the change of culture, staff engagement, care and morale became more evident, he could sense the shift of emotion, energy and focus in his home. He was being SET-UP but in this case.. to succeed. He got it!

We took the long way - we LISTENED to and ADDRESSED the staff concerns, tackled the low performers and built the morale of the team. At each supervision and weekly team meeting, I asked the team to SUPPORT the new manager. I asked them to stop the revolving door. It was within THEIR power. They agreed.

This is something that is not always clear from audits outside the immediate home- if the team support you, you have a CHANCE of winning. If there are a core that persistently don't, it will often cause the new manager to fail by

DEFAULT. This is why regularly changing a manager from the same home is often counter-productive.

In this instance, the TEAM DYNAMICS were perpetuating an environment for failure. Removing the whole team will lose you lots of skill and experience too. That is why skilful, empathic coaching to retain the talent and experience works well. It is better to isolate and challenge the unhelpful behaviours instead of simply changing the team or manager.

To summarise then, breaking the pattern required an understanding of what fed into the cocktail of a disengaged team (through supervisions and team meetings), taking control of the home and running it well (upskilling and coaching the home manager), gaining the trust and respect of the team through demonstrating competence.

Once everyone sees and feels the home working well, their feedback reinforces it - the new norm is created. The revolving door finally..finally..STOPS!.

This article is dedicated to that gentleman - you know who are. Great job. Thanks for allowing me to support you.

4.2 Reflective practice on **Does your Care / Nursing home have a "revolving door" for Home Managers? Do you want to break the pattern?**

Key themes in this article

Team dynamics and their connection with problems in care homes. Staff engagement / lack thereof. The importance of trust and integrity.

What does this article mean to you?

What can / would you apply from this learning to your practice?

Other notes

4.3 Beware! The greatest risk in your Care Home/ Healthcare facility today!

There are many we could choose – serious health and safety risks, safeguarding risks, immigration status risks of our staff, nurse PIN's expiring, fire hazards, however the risk I am referring to though is more subtle and pernicious. It reminds me of the movie ALIEN, it slowly takes over, disabling the controls, with STEALTH! What I am referring to is the influence of staff in your care home who are working AGAINST you, with a POOR ATTITUDE. To qualify this, I am not referring to your mid-range ordinary complaining, this refers to those who refuse to be managed, saying the right thing but inciting the staff team to do their own thing and discredit those running the home. These staff can be competent workers, whilst may be they are providing good care / service, the manner in which they do it and their influence can destroy your team and ruin your home or facility! Beware!

What everyone who works in this area knows is as follows; in order to create a feeling of home, staff often work autonomously in residents rooms. Often 2 will work closely together, with lots of time to chat freely. In my experience, it is this combination of work autonomy in a high trust environment, this gives space for dysfunctional team behaviours to be perpetuated by those with a poor attitude

I learnt this from experience; a couple of years ago I managed a home with 2 staff that matched this description. I addressed their attitude on various levels, it was not overt but hidden. My instinct told me they were still a type of risk - I kept a very close eye. After I had moved on, several managers later, that home was deemed "requires improvement" in all 5 areas by the CQC – (regulator). I had kept up with my former team. These 2 subversive staff were still there. I am not saying these staff were to blame but I can confidently say is that these 2 influential individuals hindered the staff team gelling, forming into a supportive, positive and engaged team. There was nothing intrinsically wrong within the home beyond the group behaviours of the team. These 2 were not the cause but they blocked healthy team behaviours developing and becoming the norm, under the leadership of the manager.

These were challenging individuals, who refused to accept responsibility for their behaviours instead blaming and inciting others to join their ranks. Upon reflection, would I do it any different? No, but I would have benefitted from a coaching tool around values that separates job performance from the required behaviours for the team members. It would have been helpful to concisely give that feedback in order to try to effect specific behaviour / attitudinal change. That would have been more targeted. I will give this to you free in the next article.

In the meantime, let's look at what you can do to protect your team and home from these behaviours (weeds) taking hold in your home and ruining your team.

Firstly recruitment – recruit on attitude, with the capability to absorb or demonstrate skills. Don't compromise EVER!

Secondly, pick up the small things, the casual rudeness or poor attitude, give feedback, be encouraging, want better for them and for the service. Be a catalyst for better.

Thirdly, re-iterate the positive culture of working with a good attitude continually, reinforce through 1 to 1, team meetings, embed this culture relentlessly.

In conclusion, to protect your team and create effective service delivery requires strong leadership - both preventative and proactive. It requires discernment to understand where this happening and sensitivity and balanced feedback to help your team adapt.

Our residents and their families, our service users and commissioners all need our services to be the very best and good teamwork is crucial to effective service delivery. Let us not be weary in well-doing. They are depending on us. Let's do this.

4.3 Reflective practice on **Beware! The greatest risk in your Care Home/Healthcare facility today!**

Key themes in this article

How poor attitude from staff can spread across a care home. How this affects morale, then teamwork, then care and ultimately has a devastating effect on the home.

What does this article mean to you?

What can / would you apply from this learning to your practice?

Other notes

4.4 Managing the "greatest risk in your care home" today

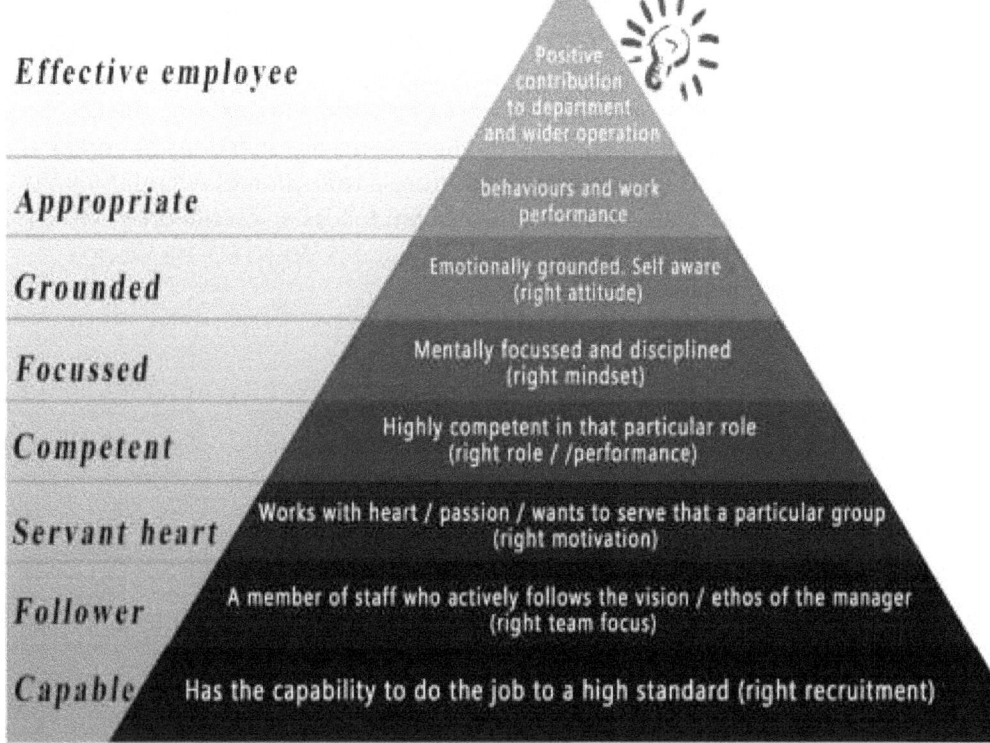

This is a follow up to my previous article, 4th Jan entitled "Beware! The greatest risk in your Care Home/ Healthcare facility today!". I promised a coaching model to help – see above.

Whilst this model is experiential, it is a reflection of care based staff that have made a positive contribution in my teams. It is designed to clearly distinguish the building blocks of a strong performer so that an intervention can be accurate, balanced and positive. It is a tool for constructive feedback. It came about after I worked with some highly capable staff who also made problems in my team. I developed the tool to equip me to be more effective with similar staff.

There are similarities to other industries but the model is based on a need for compassion led practice and for those working autonomously in a highly-regulated environment, with high degrees of transparency, accountability. There are unique vulnerabilities as a home manager (and in the UK as a CQC registered manager) which this model seeks to address. This is through equipping the manager to take a proactive approach and give feedback on the areas they wish the staff member to raise performance and reflect upon.

The overall ethos is inspired by the work of Marshall Rosenberg, the US psychologist who defined interpersonal problems as reflections of unmet and un-articulated needs. The model is therefore a reflection of what I think the needs are. In this regard, it moves away from focussing on the problems to instead focussing on the needs, a focus on what IS WANTED. His work is called NVC – non-violent communication.

4.4 Reflective practice on **Managing the "greatest risk in your care home" today**

Key themes in this article

Illustrating how good attitude from staff coupled with positive behaviours leads to more effective employees which makes for better teamwork and engagement which in turn makes a care home run more safely and effectively

What does this article mean to you?

What can / would you apply from this learning to your practice?

Other notes

4.5 Care Home Manager – (still?) best job in the world! Reflections 2 years on.

I penned my original article entitled "Care Home Manager - best job in the world" in Dec 2014. These last 2 years have given me space to reflect on the vicissitudes of the care sector, as a manager, consultant, author and coach to other home managers. I thought it would be interesting to reflect on that initial glow. Like comparing an engaged couple to those married, it is experience that often provides the richest insights;

There are 3 main forces that have changed the care landscape from 2 years ago – the CQC regulation is far more stringent. On some levels this is good and depending on the operator, can also mean a real sense of stress /job insecurity at others. This is due to (in many instances) the outcome of the inspection becoming the sole criterion for a job well done by the registered manager, a myopic focus at best.

The second force is of course the financial pressure – from the minimum wage increase and where contractors for publicly funded residents refuse to accept these cost of care increases. This brings greater financial pressure, with declining profit margins. This means care home operators are less attractive investments, making it more difficult to refinance / raise finance at good rates.

The third force (for nursing homes) a chronic shortage of nurses which has several effects – it puts intolerable pressure on contacted nurses when a home runs mainly on agency nurses. It massively increases costs – nursing homes need a minimum of qualified nurses at all times, otherwise the home is in breach. This is an issue that takes some years to resolve through training more nurses.

In my view, whatever happens operationally is a reflection of the governance, staffing structures and values and culture of the leadership of the organisation. I have written much about the importance of strong leadership at a home level- taking charge, developing teams but now I turn my focus to the design of the support structures to make care great and pay its way.

There are 2 proactive approaches to take when the going gets tough; either it is call to rethink some of the paradigms, to re-engineer some of our tasks, paperwork, and governance. It is call to be better. This is the higher view. I know you can guess where is going! Yes, the other call is to simply strip out cost and often reduce quality.

Some examples from other managers taking the cost reduction road are simply to delayer the organisation. The impact of this will depend on how these layers contributed to the registered manager maintaining quality / managing risk. Where the layers did contribute, quality may go down and risks increase. The exceptions are where there has been a comparable investment to redefine IT, information systems to offset this loss of human capital. Maybe it is necessary, but for those who have put our hearts into our work, it can be a SAD turn.

As for radical re-engineering, I haven't heard of a Dyson / Stelios / Steve Jobs equivalent in care. Obviously the south-east has the greatest demand for high end care homes with the relative cost of houses meaning it is more affordable. These South East specific operators are not immune to these forces but cossetted somewhat by strong private resident demand.

I remember a former mentor of mine who used to run private hospitals, he said that as the organisation faced daunting financial pressures, it was time to move out, then come back another time, when it is more financially robust.

I didn't fully grasp what my mentor meant. I see now that he foresaw a reduction of quality where resources are not in place to sustainably balance customer expectations, quality with staff support. On the outside very little is changed but there will be a paralysis of investment and opportunity with risk and a possible shift to a blame based / more political culture. It doesn't hurt to identify the season, summer has turned to winter. It WILL pass. In the meantime, I have moved my attention to more integrated healthcare models which are delivering more positive resident experiences right now.

Regardless of these pressures, the times are a call to leadership. Those of you who have read my articles are familiar with this call. I make no apology for repeating myself. It does not cost money to prioritise the resident, to focus on service, value. It does not cost to move our focus from a good inspection to instead a well-run home, which will naturally have a good inspection.

These are still many, many wonderful homes run by smart operators who pay well, treat their staff well, have a good governance model and supportive culture, even despite these storms. Care is a wonderful place to work. Often thankless and exhausting but to touch another person, to share their life, their last few years is a treasure that cannot be bought.

I have that treasure – it changed my life. Made my life richer, more meaningful. Like being touched by an angel, you are never the same, often with a greater humanity and respect for life. I only wish there was a greater focus on empathy within senior management. In my view, the sector doesn't need more skilled cost cutters or tough generals but rather more compassionate and entrepreneurial leaders.

Care Home Manager – best job in the world? In many instances, still YES.

4.5 Reflective practice on **Care Home Manager – (still?) best job in the world! Reflections 2 years on.**

Key themes in this article

Reviewing the 3 forces that have changed care over the last 2 years. How reducing total care costs too fast or too ambitiously can often lead to a pervasive deterioration in care quality

What does this article mean to you?

What can / would you apply from this learning to your practice?

Other notes

Part 5 – breaking taboos, leadership secrets, dear boss trilogy and in pursuit of outstanding..

Part 5 overview –

We have some in depth topics that follows which form building blocks and reference points for more complex themes to follow.

To start then, we talk about the great taboo – I think this matters to each of us on many levels – for both empathy with those who've lost a parent and also to understand that our emotional life is tied in with our life experience – let us face our fears only when we feel ready to do so.

Next is an awkwardly named article about leadership secrets – this space is so full of cliché and over promise, I found it nearly impossible to keep this in the book. It's a theme that marks out the very successful and those who effectiveness is fleeting. Hope you enjoy it!

After that, we have a trilogy of articles based on "Dear boss…". We cover 3 angles, with 3 articles but they are one – namely boss behaviour that impacts staff commitment, health and in some instances mental health. We unpick this on some levels- it is rife in the workplace but surely in the health and social care we need to do better? It's vocational work that requires the heart and soul of the staff, surely for their sake, we can support our committed staff more effectively?

Lastly I visit 2 homes rated overall CQC outstanding – I consider how much better, if at all are these highly rated homes. Have a look and see what you think.

Part 5 contents

5.1 Home Manager / Breaking the taboo on d****. **PG 121**

5.2 Care Home Manager - leadership secrets for CONSISTENT success - identifying the one key personal quality we all need. **PG 125**

5.3 Dear boss, my commitment to you was lost today. This is why... **PG 129**

5.4 Dear boss, working for you is affecting my health. This is why...**PG 133**

5.5 Dear boss, working in this organisation is affecting my MENTAL HEALTH. This is why...**PG 137**

5.6 Care Home Manager / how much better is a CQC rated "outstanding" home? Reflections from 2 visits in December. **PG 141**

5.1 Care Home Manager / Breaking the taboo on d****. Supporting the grieving.

In many ways, this is the article I feared most to write and therefore, the one I must write. A fear to be confronted. I avoided sharing this a year ago and yet this event will befall us all. It is part of the cycle of family life. Whilst we do not embrace death, loss or grief, perhaps it is better to acknowledge its place, to rob it of that power to surprise? With that in mind courageous readers, let us press on.

You see, 1 year ago today my mother left this world. She had an accident. We found her the next morning at home at 6am. Bleary eyed, I made the 999 calls, the family calls, dealt with the police and the undertakers, saw my mother out of the house, whilst waiting with her. Within 5 hours, we went from normal family life to this new undefined territory. The working out of this change would take some time. The last major change to this unit was the addition of a new child 44 years ago. A smiley, third child with long legs (yours truly). Their love started bravely 57 years ago, a 16 year old and 20 year smitten, full of hope. Children, marriages and grand-kids were proudly added over the years and yet it remained constant. It stopped without warning, 1 year ago today.

As someone who is generally optimistic, I found death an uneasy and puzzling companion. It resisted my attempts at positive reframing. Nearly every problem or challenge I have encountered can be redefined, can give power if interpreted more helpfully. Death defied my strategies. It was fearless and unapologetic, violent and impolite. It was no respecter of person. It was check mate, game over.

The primary emotional states I experienced were shock and denial, intermingled with grief and loss. Topped off with trauma from the very practical aspects of death – vivid images that persisted in the mind, till help was sought. It was a veritable cocktail of complex emotions and states. This grief felt like riding a wave. Like riding a way either one stayed in control or was enveloped by grief. It took effort to process these emotions and not be overwhelmed by it.

Shock was the first emotion but I knew the more I blocked it, the more these intense emotions would rock me to the very core of my being. The only way to reduce this intense sense of being out of control was to ACCEPT IT. Whatever I did, I could not turn the clock back. The desire for 1 more day with my beautiful mother was overwhelming. Acceptance would save me from this all consuming loss and grief. ACCEPTANCE was sanity.

What was surprising was how we moved from 1 life to another as our family changed – it had happened on us. Suddenly we had to explain to everyone or hold this secret in. It was a profound change, an awakening, a sobering up, an ending and later a beginning. The nucleus of family and friends gradually regrouped and reshaped. The family found new reference points, was redefined individually and collectively. Slowly and gingerly, with much trepidation, cautiously, self-consciously. one foot in front of another, the family started to LIVE again. There was no other palatable choice, though there were other choices. We all had the gift of life. We were lucky. We were ALIVE.

At the time, it redefined friendships; old friends stepped up who had been through the same, showed their love, other friends recoiled with discomfort. It was a strange time. I was advised to get a grief counsellor and I did so for a short time. Did it help? Kind of. Whilst a safe place to explore, it was also strange. One time, we overran by a few minutes (she was particular), She nearly threw me out of her house! Her strict adherence to time keeping took priority over my feelings and my grief. She was a supervisor Counsellor and yet had no EMPATHY, just reassuring sounds and nods. It is a rare quality indeed. I am still grateful for the emotional space she gave me. Imperfect can also be ok.

For a short while after, I entered this strange world of comfort from all sides, from my neighbour to many people I hardly spoke to. Much of it saved me. Like a bucket wholly empty with holes in, some of those words and expressions of care, reconnected me to life, to mankind, to our shared bond, our shared humanity. For a moment we were all together, it was a profound experience of needing and people instinctively understanding that the normalising of the grief is needed, really needed. I was touched and it shook my view of the world, my view of me and others. Life was not as black and white or single dimensional as I thought. It was infinitely richer and more complex.

For a short while after, I had so many telling me "she was still there, still with me". It was a stretch of my personal and private beliefs. I resisted judgement, just listened. I did have some undefined experiences of that uncoupling of the umbilical cord, whether spiritual, emotional or other, I know not. Yes it does occur in some way, beyond words. I am comfortable to leave it undefined. In my view, there is a realm of the sacred, beyond religion, where words are poor representations of experience. That is enough for me.

During this year, I processed my private grief, allowed myself to regroup, to reform. I realised that death is something to neither be proud of or shy away from, it simply IS and that's OK. I was lucky I was able to put my arm around my mum the day she died. Our last words were sharing a joke. We ended on love. I am grateful for that.

When we consider that this will befall us and our parents, there is only 1 response to death only 1 force can hinder its stealth, can sweeten our life's journey. It is of course LOVE. Not sentimental, or schmaltzy love but rather a mature appreciation and response to the value of every life. Faces may not show it, words may deny it but all those you see and spend time with all need your love. Can you see it now? Don't delay.

Dedicated to all those who support those who have lost a parent.

5.1 Reflective practice on **Care Home Manager / Breaking the taboo on d****. Supporting the grieving.**

Key themes in this article

Facing the death of a parent. The grieving process. Offering empathy to families over the loss of their parent.

What does this article mean to you?

What can / would you apply from this learning to your practice?

Other notes

5.2 Care Home Manager - leadership secrets for CONSISTENT success - identifying the one key personal quality we all need

Friends, for those of who know me well, I may take a year or more to chew over some nugget of information, looking for patterns and trends. The whole "secrets of success" is a crowded space of ideas and thoughts but bear with me - this is about insight and comes from an extraordinarily successful businessman - there is a nugget of truth about effective leadership and commercial success which may be worth a few minutes of your time. I hope you find it helpful;

I just finished reading a book by a remarkable man and found what was I looking for. The gentleman is called Terry Leahy – for 15 years, he was CEO of Tesco (the Billion £ retailer). What was remarkable about his 15 years was that he had a CONTINUALLY growing business quarter by quarter for the whole period! In recession and otherwise, EVERY SINGLE QUARTER! This gentleman's success suggests there is something radical and powerful, a different paradigm he is using to get such consistent results. Are you curious to know what it is?

Let's continue – in the book "Management in 10 words", Mr Leahy explains his management style in 10 words are "Truth, loyalty, courage, values, act, balance, simple, lean, compete, trust" – a nice mixture of enlightened management thinking delivered with integrity and consistency but still I wondered, what was it? How come he achieved this radical consistent success? He gives a hint when he talks about "managers lacking a basic humanity" – page 297 and saved the bombshell for page 299, the last page where he says, "if I had to choose which of the ten words is the most important, I would say TRUTH" – he explained it was being true to oneself (integrity) and also seeking and speaking the truth. BINGO! There we have it. I accept this may be an on obscure reference but bear with me;

Firstly, in terms of lessons for leaders, personal integrity is a must – without this, according to Mr Leahys work, continual success is unlikely. Coupled with this MUST be an obsession with truth – an open mind, searching. In practice, this is not being too attached to our own views, listening if someone has something that challenges our views - knowing when to take it on board, not block it. For some, it may also be listening to your conscience telling you to say or do something different and that voice being blocked as the "truth" is uncomfortable. In my humble opinion, it is this grappling and yielding and the moral strength and clarity it brings which prepares someone for success with others - they've won the battle with themselves.

I believe this combination works as personal integrity gives congruence and the ability to connect deeply – when coupled with a low ego / desire for truth, you have a literal WINNING FORMULA. Don't mistake authenticity with integrity – anyone can truthfully tell you their mistaken idea, with a clean conscience! BE DISCERNING friends!

When I reflect on some truly great CEO's I've known- there a few that come to mind in manufacturing, care, social housing- yes they did have these qualities, this holds true in my experience.

Friends, this is deep but in my experience, true principles often are. There you have it – a winning formula for success from a great man. Let's all strive to achieve this consistent success by modelling these behaviours – let's champion personal integrity in our professional friendships, let's speak the truth to each other, even if it hurts (timing, diplomacy and good sense, cultural sensitivity and awareness still apply of course)– these are sure ways to inspire each other to greater, CONSISTENT SUCCESS. I am in – are you?

5.2 Reflective practice on **Care Home Manager - leadership secrets for CONSISTENT success - identifying the one key personal quality we all need**

Key themes in this article

Telling the "truth" versus political manoeuvring is linked to consistent high performance. This is the opposite of a perfectionist mindset / managing appearances. This can only happen across all strata of a company if the behaviour is modelled and sustained by key company figures. It's subtle and rare.

What does this article mean to you?

What can / would you apply from this learning to your practice?

Other notes

5.3 Dear boss, my commitment to you was lost today. This is why...

I bumped into a former boss of mine at a trade show, an austere gentleman now in his mid sixties. We exchanged pleasantries and caught up briefly, he looked slightly uncomfortable. I recall he wasn't a particularly likeable gentleman, rather highly strung, if memory serves me well? We had worked together for 2 years. It brought me straight back to my experiences working for him and the point where our working relationship changed. This is the part I want to reflect on today;

In our first 4 months we were in a honeymoon period, we were different but accepting of the differences, there was a relationship of a sort, there was trust, like friends from afar, we worked together with a shared respect and goodwill. I felt supported. I took great efforts to help and support him in turn. That was until an appraisal changed things between us.

Before you race ahead, it wasn't what you may think. I was used to performance reviews, I enjoyed celebrating the successes. This one was different, it wasn't bad at all but I noticed something, he winced at one thing that wasn't done and made light of the long list of worthy successes. He did not celebrate, smile, encourage, or affirm these things AT ALL. The appraisal was objective but more a judgement based on few facts. It was perfunctory, it served its purpose but that was the day our relationship changed.

It changed because I now understood we did not have a relationship. It changed because I realised the extra work and effort was not acknowledged and wouldn't be rewarded. Crucially, I began to learn that any deviation from any tittle of any instruction would be met with anger. I slowly began to realise that I had unknowingly entered a control based work relationship, fear was the primary motivator. It was the over-used cliche of using a stick to manage somebody and use it they did! It was so old fashioned - I hadn't expected it from this brand.

Over the coming year, I would see him crush others with public shame and expectations that were wholly unrealistic. The commendable notion of the "drive them hard, make them work" professional dissipated as I saw first-hand the impact of his working style on others. It was driving extra hard permanently, BECAUSE HE COULD. It didn't sit well with me.

I saw the aggression and unflinching accountability required on every detail and yet when he didn't deliver things on time, he just explained it away. It was clear there was another set of rules for him. Reason had no place, the rules were the rules, context had no bearing, only submission mattered. It was a command and control situation – we were there to be told. Like a scene out of the movie "1984". It was nearly funny- until it started to affect me.

I slowly realised that most of the dead-lines imposed HAD NO REAL PURPOSE. It was just a lack of planning in advance on his side. I saw colleagues gain weight through chronic overworking, go temporarily crazy with the stress. It was like a mission and yet a pointless one. It wasn't customers we were fighting for, or the business. So it begs the question, what we were striving for, suffering for?

Unknowingly, it seems we were being forced to confirm the business view this guy had, like a blunt hammer with the nails being the operational challenges that popped up day by day. At times, the narrative and solutions didn't fit, but no matter he said, just KEEP FOLLOWING MY LEAD. It was leadership but a de-humanising form of it.

I left a year or two later, I adjusted, but I never did the extra work he first enjoyed. I became guarded/ we achieved some modest goals but we didn't achieve anything GREAT. During that time, he was under considerable stress, the more he tried to control my team was the more stressed he became. Under pressure, he became even more unyielding. I felt a bit sorry for him but couldn't help him, he was unaware of all these dynamics but utterly convinced he KNEW IT ALL. He couldn't be helped. It seemed he was in a prison of his own making.

I believe he had a mild heart attack some time later. Of course, it is common knowledge these behaviours actually make people SICK. In my view, trying to control everyone and becoming exhausted when it doesn't quite work is a psychological maladjustment. Passive aggression can be every bit as damaging as more overt forms.

This brings me to my final point; thinking about how common this in the workplace and then reflecting on the scale of this WASTE of HUMAN CAPITAL and the impact this has on organisations up and down the country and society as a whole.

Do these passive aggressive / aggressive leaders not realise that when staff are treated as an object, a resource, they will withdraw, that engagement and commitment will suffer? It really is an organisational "own goal".

I liken these fear based management approaches to an interaction between lovers, where out of the blue, one hits the other round the face and then wonders why the mood changes! Passive aggression in the workplace is rife, like casual violence, it violates those it touches. Relationships are never the same after.

In my view, we are not RESOURCES caught in an industrial machine, the time for that metaphor has passed. We need an updated paradigm of work which releases the human capital we have. We need a new paradigm of collaboration and trust, free from fear.

This is why I have a passion for talking about leadership with integrity, introducing people to self-awareness, the power of empathy and compassion based leadership, especially within social care. I love these things because they work. I love them because they are humanising

In the mean-time, who will raise the bar and lead by example in the workplace? I know my behaviours impact the culture where I work, it's a big responsibility, requiring our very best. Who would be a leader? In my view, there is a power for good in leading and managing well. Mistreating the staff is a cheap and short sighted tactic. It will always harm the business in the end and diminish the standing of the leader.

5.3 Reflective practice on **Dear boss, my commitment to you was lost today. This is why...**

Key themes in this article

Workplace bullying. It can be subtle and indirect but it is very common. How the line manager treats their direct report. The psychology of a controlling manager. The waste of human capital.

What does this article mean to you?

What can / would you apply from this learning to your practice?

Other notes

5.4 Dear boss, working for you is affecting my health. This is why.

I am grateful to a coaching client of mine who has allowed me to share their story. You know who you are, THANK YOU.

I recently published an article "Dear boss, my commitment to you was lost today, this is why." It illustrated management behaviours that lead to **EMPLOYEE DISENGAGEMENT**. Over this article and the next, I continue this look at the loss of human capital and some of the management behaviours that perpetuate it. This article develops the idea further from a line manager to team member perspective. That the experience is so common in organisations is not news but that WE CONTINUE TO ALLOW IT on our organisations, despite an awareness of the cost, is surely worth considering;'

Firstly dis-engaging staff is counter intuitive, companies recruit the best, want the best from their people, then in some cases, much of that energy and talent dissipates through the behaviours of (some) bosses and through the company culture. A bit like a radiator that needs bleeding, the heating is on but it's not getting through at the point of need. In these organisations, the directors are often unaware of the culture they perpetuate (root cause) and many competent staff leave because of these 2 cross-winds of manager behaviours and company culture. (outcome of the combination).

Secondly, in a time of recovering prosperity across the world post 2008, a loss of productivity, unnecessary attrition, and the resulting waste of human capital are not just abstract concepts, they are tangible and pressing concerns. Surprisingly, only a small number of leaders seems to instinctively grasp the link between this lost human capital and the success of their organisation. Anyway, I digress. back to the subject, the dissipating of talent through staff disengagement in its many forms, firstly though, back to the **UNAWARE BOSS**;

I coached this lady for 3 months, she was being **bullied at work** during this time and we worked through these issues until she was clear on what was best for her. My client lost 1 stone, stopped eating, had disturbed sleep, had to use medication to just keep functioning and she did, she later fought the bullying with a grievance. She eventually decided to move on.

Her team loved her, she had made a demonstrable impact in her area. Like many before her (attrition was high), she declined an exit interview with an employer that **didn't seem to want to hear** what was going wrong. We used the experience to make her strong but it left a scar. In my experience this scale of breach of trust can take some time to heal.

So, why you may ask did working for this boss make my client sick (or contribute to it) and were there any reasonable grounds for her boss to treat her this way? I don't know all the facts, I am basing my views on our meetings, visiting her workplace and talking to a few of her team. What I could glean however was that **her team considered she was doing well and in terms of metrics she was performing well**, so there was a disconnect here between that and her boss's perception.

The common themes that came up from her boss's feedback was a subjective level of discomfort but **NO SPECIFICS**. It was apparent she was building a case against her and misusing the company's disciplinary process to do so. There was no identification of unmet needs / training needs or needs for mentoring, just a hazy judgement, a withdrawal of support and aggression played out with a threat of disciplinary action. My client left the business and therefore her grievance was not concluded. It is unlikely there was any action taken against this aggressor yet shouldn't there be? We will look at these cultural / organisational forces at work in the next article. In the meantime,

What made my client sick then?

Impossible deadlines without the ability to influence them. Not being listened to. Not being understood. Lack of support. A lack of authentic conversation about the root causes of issues within her workplace and the necessary support to address them. **The need to maintain the boss's narrative overruled the reality she faced.** In short, an authoritarian management style of a manager lacking personal awareness.

What can be done to address these poor practices within industry? 5 things come to mind;

1) I think training can play a part but so much of this is UNCONSCIOUSLY played out.

There could be an anti-bullying workshop for managers and how it plays out, but few would identify their tough, unyielding style as contributing to a perception of bullying. It is **SUBTLE.**

Coaching skills with self-awareness and empathy are core competencies to avoid this. Also training on personality profiling and how to manage those of a different profile may help.

2) Ensuring the top leaders have a line of regular direct communication to middle managers may help.

3) The most **senior leaders set the tone** in the organisation, by OMISSION OR COMMISSION. In my view, it reveals a need for strong, SELF AWARE leadership to address these habitual behaviours. 360-degree appraisals are a tool that can provide measured feedback and partially shift the manager to employee POWER IMBALANCE.

4) **The existing HR tools are LIMITED.** Staff surveys are not in real-time and can be ambiguous. Grievance and disciplinaries are blunt tools to align needs and foster more constructive working relationships. Some form of staff empowerment to flag the lower-level bullying behaviours (before they escalate) may contain this.

5) **Ownership**. Who owns this stuff at an organisational level? The importance of staff engagement and culture impacts all parts of the business. A senior director needs to drive the debate and company accountability for reviewing policy and progress toward this end.

Hope that was of interest. We will look at the part the organisation plays in the next article.

5.4 Reflective practice on **Dear boss, working for you is affecting my health. This is why.**

Key themes in this article

The link between the line manager relationship and their physical health. Company culture and the normalising of coercive behaviours. The root cause is often managers who lack self-awareness and a degree of emotional intelligence.

What does this article mean to you?

What can / would you apply from this learning to your practice?

Other notes

5.5 Dear boss, working in this organisation is affecting my MENTAL HEALTH. This is why.

Dear readers, this is third in the trilogy of articles on addressed to "Dear boss...". The previous 2 articles looked at how a manager can affect staff engagement and in some cases inadvertently make their staff unwell through their management style. This 3rd article moves onto how company CULTURE can impact the mental and emotional well-being of STAFF. Though some may see this as a taboo, in my experience as a psychotherapist, I found that many mental health issues take root through denial and pretence, I think we should at least consider the possibility of a link.

Whilst these dynamics are not limited to health and social care, in my view the staff that provide healthcare and emotional care especially need to be emotionally and mentally supported due to the nature of the work. Hope that makes sense, let's continue.

Whilst working as a consultant, I coached a new manager and his team running a care home in the North of England. It surprised me that 3 of his new staff had developed mental health issues working there, under the previous boss. I met with these staff members and did some coaching with them. It quickly became clear that the mental health issues seemed to have developed from their work and secondly that they ALL had no previous experiences of mental health issues.

I wondered, could it be a co-incidence or worse, could it be that the management style together with the culture brought this on? It's a radical idea I know. The manager part was covered in the last article. Whilst this is not an article about mental health issues (a broad subject), we touch on the fringes of it here. There is a welcome focus in society being more accepting about those experiencing mental health issues (think Prince Harry, Ruby Wax, Stephen Fry) but WHAT IF the culture and workplace are bringing it on? What if "the problem" was not mental health issues but more ineffective management / leadership? It's a sobering thought isn't it?

Back to the 3 staff members with mental health issues, between them, there had been suicidal tendencies, 2 of the 3 had been on medical anti-depressants. Whether these individuals had a predisposition to mental health issues is not clear but what we do know is that they all manifested under this manager and secondly that the cultural forces made it worse. I know this because I coached them, they were offered support and care and got better. I know this because under their new boss, they no longer exhibited these issues and still don't several years on (I still get the odd thank you e mail from our work together.).

Let's break this down a bit more - for each of them their experience was very personal, they didn't share it and there is no obvious way to address it within the workplace apart from perhaps a helpline which is not connected to those who run the business, the culture or the manager. For someone experiencing floods of tears, irrational thoughts with low self-esteem it can be very hard to identify what is clearly happening. They may feel it is their problem / weakness etc. It is hard for them to outline the connection though they may instinctively feel it. Instead, they suffered in silence.

In my view, the cultural forces played a part as some of their role expectations were too rigid and unrealistic. These expectations came from a management culture that didn't engage or listen or come up with new solutions. It was an old fashioned, command and control set-up. So along with bullying and intimidation from the previous manager, these forces made it a whole lot worse. The staff felt powerless, became compliant. Their creativity and drive consumed by trying to look good. They worked for an organisation doing a great work BUT who were on some levels not yet a GREAT EMPLOYER.

In my experience the company culture develops from a set of norms and positions on things, precedents that become the established way. The trouble builds when poor decisions are made (e.g. jobs given to the weakest candidate because of favouritism) or senior jobs given to those who just keep the status quo and block out anything uncomfortable, this builds trouble over time as employees perceive that survival is the real game being played out. Contrary to the stated mission, it is NOT great service, not excellence, not teamwork that matters. FATALLY for the organisation, they simply ADAPT.

There are 3 things that keep this status quo- firstly boards who keep recruiting leaders with little emotional intelligence – this outcome will be inevitable with this profile of leaders (unless they have a deputy leader who has these traits or another corresponding balance in another role). Secondly, the leaders surround themselves with career professionals with exactly the same outlook (short-listing / profiling / recruitment needs broadening.). Thirdly, there is no early warning system to highlight breaches of behaviour by senior managers against the company values. A grievance is usually too late and whistle-blowing is too strong. Both can be career limiting. The start of these unconstructive forces is often more subtle, like a weed in a garden that grows quickly. It needs addressing quickly by strong leaders with clear values and clear accountability for maintaining high standards of integrity and support.

In conclusion, in some cases, a poor management style combined with a management culture can make staff sick, "feel crazy" as they struggle to meet impossible demands and feel despondent and powerless when they fail. It is tempting to personalise it but in the end the company culture is the reflection of what the leader allows and supports by omission or commission. All roads lead back to the leader who sets the tone. This is why I think educating health and social care leaders in the art of listening, empathy, and compassion led care are so important.

There are some amazing leaders in social care that I have had the privilege to meet and work with and look up to. I hope this article will give courage to those leaders struggling with these issues to get some expert input. It is in all our interests to make our health and social care organisations great places to work, so our teams can provide the care our residents and patients deserve.

5.5 Reflective practice on **Dear boss, working in this organisation is affecting my MENTAL HEALTH. This is why**

Key themes in this article

The link between working for line managers who are authoritarian with poor boundaries and how their power misused can bring out mental health issues (expressed as low level psychosis and acting out / overeating / alcohol misuse / depression etc) with their direct reports.

What does this article mean to you?

What can / would you apply from this learning to your practice?

Other notes

5.6 Care Home Manager / how much better is a CQC rated "outstanding" home?. Reflections from 2 visits in December.

Dear readers, friends and former colleagues, I just wanted to sneak this article in before the Christmas break, while the material is still fresh in my mind. Two weeks ago, I visited two large care homes with an overall CQC rating of "outstanding". I visited to learn from the best. What I found surprised and confounded me in equal measure. It's a broad and complex subject, so let me cover off a few fundamentals to start;

The Quest for "outstanding"

The quest to achieve an overall CQC rating of "outstanding" is the stated goal of most care home operators, whether private or not for profit. This means concerning the 5 CQC questions of **Is the service "safe, caring, effective, well led and responsive?"**, the overall rating given is "outstanding." As of todays CQC website (24/12/17), the recent ratings for care home inspections are 18 "outstanding" **(2.5%)**, 400 good **(55%)**, 236 "requires improvement" **(33%)**, 65 rated "inadequate" **(9%)**.

Analysis / snapshot.

Analysis of this data shows, **42% of homes inspected are not meeting the CQC standards** and 2.5% are on the very top, excelling. This suggests the greater challenge for the care home sector is to move the 42% not meeting standards ("**requires improvement**" and "**inadequate**") towards a rating of "good". At the same time, the challenge is for the 55% rated "good" to retain this rating and for the very best to stretch toward the ultimate rating of "outstanding."

I would make the obvious point that a rating of "outstanding" is relative to "good" so statistically it is likely to remain a fairly small part (I stand to be corrected here.) As a current home manager my guiding principle is to run the home 24/7 in such a way that it would be deemed at least "good" in all areas if there was an impromptu CQC inspection. For most homes, in my view, the work to achieve and retain an "outstanding" rating is of a different magnitude and I will touch on this below.

Notes from the 2 visits

I digress, back to these 2 visits - these were 2 homes of 6 run by a not for profit provider. Statistically, having 33% of your homes (albeit a small number) is interesting! Furthermore, in 2015 and 2017, one of these homes received a rating of "outstanding" under the stewardship of the same manager. Now, that is VERY interesting, isn't it?

It took 2 days of my leave and 8 hours of driving to meet these extraordinary leaders and their teams. I left genuinely inspired (an overused word I know!). What did I notice? Here are a few things that stand out;

Their facilities and ethos for dementia care were breath-taking. There was so much best practice in place; it would take several articles to articulate. The staffing ratios for this part of the service were relatively high (to industry norms) and the facilities were generous and comfortable. however, it was the leadership, teamwork and ethos both of which brought it to life. The staff all lived and breathed it as a cohesive team. They may not use these words but this is what I noticed. It's a feeling and a reality, more than a management description. It is the point where language starts to fall short of describing an experience.

In both cases, the Home Manager and deputy were a tightly knit team and in both homes the sense of leadership extended to a further level of leaders within the home. It was a team approach; it wasn't simply a case of a sole "superstar" creating this magic. The leaders were very clear to make this distinction though they were both exceptional **managers** and **leaders** in their own right. I use both terms as they both secured the engagement of the team (leadership) and managed well (management -effective controls, administration and governance.)

Lastly, I noticed that when asked "what made the home or service outstanding?", (wait for it), they didn't know! Before you berate me for that ant-climax, hold on. Other senior figures in the UK care home industry have expressed the same truth to me, "if only we could bottle what that particular manager does like a magic elixir, we would!" I think this is fascinating and goes to the heart of the discussion around what makes a home "outstanding." I will confine my conclusions to what I am sure about;

Conclusions

These homes and the people who run them weren't "perfect" but they were well run and by implication, meeting the CQC outcome of "well led". This was very evident.

Each home took the principles of "person centred care" to a whole new level which is easier to see and experience than describe. The home wasn't about them at all. They were leaders who really did put the residents first in all things – in their management style and in the practices and team behaviours within the home.

The sense of teamwork and engagement was also tangible, natural and had developed over time. It wasn't a fad or new initiative, they lived it very day. I think that is why it is so hard to define what makes a home or a team that leads a home as "outstanding."

To answer the question then "How much better is a CQC rated "outstanding" home, I would say that they are tangibly better than a home rated simply "good", although some of the differences are subtle. In my view, It is as much about what they do as what they don't do that makes their recipe for outstanding work. I know that's vague but that's exactly how subtle the differences are.

5.6 Reflective practice on **5.6 Care Home Manager / how much better is a CQC rated "outstanding" home? Reflections from 2 visits in December.**

Key themes in this article

Defining the quest, analysis and the paradox of trying to understand what makes it "outstanding".

What does this article mean to you?

What can / would you apply from this learning to your practice?

Other notes

Part 6 – care home accountability, the "s" word, turning services / a blind eye

Part 6 overview

In our final part to the book, we explore some complex themes with many variables, building on themes already discussed earlier in the book.

To start then, we look at care home accountability and consider both organisational and legal accountability and where they cross-over and the implications of this.

Next we consider staff objections to promote private beds and break these down and offer some alternative beliefs for care staff to embrace. A financially successful home is needed to serve our communities better and to have a sustainable service

After this, with a context of an emerging market for specialists to deal with problem care homes, we consider which can be turned and which can't and identify some variables to help identify the barriers and markers for success.

Finally, we end with a call to have that difficult conversation and yet it is so much more than a conversation – it is leadership, having standards, stepping up, doing the unpopular and uncomfortable stuff. This grit is what distinguishes managers from leaders, the process a secret to crafting boldness and authenticity. Not for the fainthearted. Only for leaders!

Part 6 contents

6.1 ...Manager accountability - legal vs organisational. Never the t..? **PG 151**

6.2 Care Home Manager / why you shouldn't be frightened of the "S" word / tips for building your private bed occupancy. **PG 155**

6.3 Care Home Manager / which services can be turned and which can't? Reflections from supporting an owner / operator. **PG 161**

6.4 .. Home Manager / .. is it time you had that difficult conversation?**PG 165**

6.5 Care Home Manager / vocation vs job / seeing the "giants" in our midst **PG 169**

6.1 Care Home Manager accountability - legal vs organisational. Never the twain shall meet?

One of the things I love about the development of the CQC legislation on "registered manager" is that the individual is held to account for what happens in their home – by omission or commission, they will answer for what occurred. I love this because it encourages ownership and fosters leadership. I love that the buck stops with this person. They are empowered. It is a good thing – responsible and forward thinking yes BUT what about the rest of those above the home manager? I know there is a responsible nominated individual assigned who will also be held to account but..here it comes, **what about those in the middle?**

Before some unscrupulous readers assume a negative intent here - there is none. I have worked for and served many care home groups with some remarkable senior managers in place. I am simply making the point that regardless of their ability there is a slight disconnect between the home managers with legal accountability and those more senior managers who **make decisions about direction / resource allocation without this responsibility**. The CQC is aware of this and reviewing this matter. In the meantime here are a few thoughts about the limitations and vulnerabilities of the current system;

The registered home manager is fully responsible for taking action to ensure the home is compliant but what if those above do not offer support – how does the registered home manager exercise their responsibilities then? What do you do if the support structure doesn't agree to what's needed? This is where the legal vs organisational accountability conflict occurs. I wonder if the care home management structures have evolved sufficiently to enable the registered managers' to do their job.

The least effective support structures I've come across have had the following characteristics – senior managers holding the RM accountable to extreme levels of rigour, without any accountability themselves and occasionally with passive aggressive behaviours. I've encountered senior managers being subjective without reviewing any objective data at all – e.g. well designed and executed audits or detailed resident and staff feedback. In my view, the inherent problem with this type of support is **the lack of focus and objectivity.**

The most effective support structures I've come across are just that – plainly support structures both by intent and by design. They have a spirit of support woven in. They are in response to the complex job of running a service compliant with the CQC KLOE' (key lines of enquiry - is the service well led, effective, responsive, safe, caring?)s and make it easier for the RM to do so – usefully highlighting areas for adjustment / improvement. I know some groups do full mock CQC inspections with very good actual CQC results after. There is a lot of great practice out there.

To conclude I think the sense of ownership intended by this CQC legislation focus is helpful but it needs to be married to a sense of support and an effective and responsive management structure above the registered home manager for optimal results. That way organisational accountability and legal accountability are aligned. In the end, decisions about the service should reflect the needs of the residents it serves. As an industry we mustn't allow politics to get in the way of great care.

In my view, we are all accountable aren't we?

6.1 Reflective practice on **Care Home Manager accountability - legal vs organisational. Never the twain shall meet?**

Key themes in this article

Highlighting the potential conflict between these 2 types of accountabilities from stakeholders with different needs and priorities. The need for the alignment of both for the greater good.

What does this article mean to you?

What can / would you apply from this learning to your practice?

Other notes

6.2 Care Home Manager / why you shouldn't be frightened of the "S" word / tips for building your private bed occupancy.

The "s" word is selling! Now let me be very clear who this article is written for. It is for anyone with a care home facility that has a proportion of empty private paying beds available and would like to know how to move towards fuller occupancy.

Clearly, I will need to make some broad generalisations to make the article succinct, please bear with me. I do have some principles to share that have worked for me in several different care home settings. The approach is systematic and educational in the broad sense.

Let's make a start;

Part 1 – checklist for marketability

Is there a local market for these beds? – people who want them (unmet demand) and with a budget to pay the price you've set?

Value for money? - does your care bed offer good value for money – fair market price?

Is the home attractive and homely? – does it smell clean, is it maintained to a fair standard, is there a nice "feel" to it – staff with eye contact, smiling, with residents well cared for (physically and emotionally) – is there a nice relationship between staff and residents?

Manager / seniors friendly and approachable? focussed on the residents.

Staff team seem decent and consistent? Low or no agency usage that you can discern

Local reputation? – is credible / CQC rating suggests safety, good care and sound governance.

If you have these 6, you have a sound product to market

Now let's look at how we build occupancy.

Part 2 – dealing with Staff objections

Firstly, dealing with objections to "selling" (and alternative views.)

I can't sell. (you don't need to promote the beds, you're not selling 2nd hand cars! That paradigm is out of date. Good selling is about identifying needs and meeting them).

Selling is embarrassing. (selling where you are legitimately helping another with their needs, helping them identify what is important, agreeing a relevant well priced solution. This is service at its best. You are helping a family. There is nothing embarrassing about that! Be proud of the positive difference this can make).

Care beds shouldn't need to be sold. It is all about care! (The NHS is far from free, it costs about £122 billion ((budget 2017/18)) but thankfully free at the point of use. It is in everyone's interest for a service to be financially viable so it can continue to operate, reinvest some profit / surplus and meet its financial obligations. Staff wages and suppliers need to be paid! These are weak arguments.)

It's wrong that people sell their homes to pay for care / its too expensive! (I don't wholly disagree, but I am unable to influence these things myself. I accept the system and funding is imperfect but let's work with it. My influence on public policy is limited. The vulnerable older person in front of you needs help now. If we have a room, and finance is there, we should help now.)

I am embarrassed at selling a care bed. It is too expensive!(the delivery of care – 24 hr presence, food, laundry heating, help with general living, accommodation, decorating, repairs, electric and gas, regulated and overseen for as little as £70 per day. It's expensive but remember it's an all inclusive price for living. In many cases it is great value, the same price as a downmarket hotel without food, laundry, care, and personal support! If you add up all your personal bills for accommodation, food, heating, repairs and turn it into a weekly cost, it will be more than you think!)

I don't feel care should be a profit centre / make a profit (a fair point – there are charities that do an amazing job in this space but the private sector also brings much needed capital and bed capacity to the sector. There is choice in every major town – like a home purchase or care purchase, there are different offerings for different pockets.)

Part 3 – Mindset

Ok -we've checked your offering is sound, has a market, we've dealt with unhelpful thinking and objections to "selling" your empty beds, let's move on now to some useful frames of reference to get your next enquiries;

Coaching Point 1 – Start with 1.

Start with 1. Look for 1 new resident. Don't look for 10 or 5 – the challenge is too great. Look for 1. Then...look for 1 more. The process of chunking it down makes the process far less daunting, far more doable.

Coaching Point 2 – be proud of the product and process / selling is helping

Yes there are budgets, and Profit and Loss considerations, maybe bonuses to be won and maybe there is pressure if you don't hit your numbers but none of these factors are fuel for a sale. Fear doesn't sell. You need to be excited that you can help 1 more family, think how good it would be. Provided you are legitimately selling to meet someone's needs, providing good value and a good quality of life, you're helping. Selling correctly understood is helping.

Coaching Point 3 – a positive work environment for the staff is key

You can't fake the "feel" of a place. You can't fake authentic relationships. You can't fake the feeling of confidence staff have when they are working somewhere well led, well managed with good boundaries, with reciprocal care for the staff and residents. Manage the staff as your ambassadors and usually, they will do you proud. It is what they do when you are not there that is key. This is all about relationship with the leadership team of the home, respect / trust and maintaining high standards within your home.

Coaching Point 4 – pulling it together / vision

Once you've done these things, you need a vision to share of what you are / what you want the home to be, the specialist areas, strengths, approach, underpinning values. Define what your home is, have a clear vision. In the end, once the facilities, shifts, care, activities, all are in place, it wants to feel like a home from home with an extended family. A home where all accept each other, get on, enjoy life, being loved and valued. Who wouldn't want that for their loved one?

6.2 Reflective practice on **Care Home Manager / why you shouldn't be frightened of the "S" word / tips for building your private bed occupancy.**

Key themes in this article

Breaking down the mystery of "selling care". Talking about the connection between marketability, dealing with staff objections and the importance of possessing a positive mindset with the selling and marketing of residential based care.

What does this article mean to you?

What can / would you apply from this learning to your practice?

Other notes

6.3 Care Home Manager / which services can be turned and which can't? Reflections from supporting an owner / operator.

An owner / operator reached out to me via linked-in for some advice on her struggling service. I provided some advice and recommended a care quality specialist. I stayed in touch informally and watched the strategy unfold. In supporting, I learnt the balance between optimism, pragmatism with the absolute necessity of effective and safe care. Where do they overlap? How far can change management, cultural change techniques take a struggling service? What are the limits, if any? Are there are any factors that tip the balance away from success? She eventually chose to sell up and move out of care and is I gather doing very well. I found her journey to this decision insightful. Let's see if we can learn from her experience – I've broken it down into 2 key points and 4 qualifiers;

Key point 1 – why is the service failing? In assessing whether a service can be turned, there is nearly always a story of a breakdown of trust and credibility. It usually focuses on the work of the manager. The narrative will often have hardened. A service poorly run is an emotive matter but equally there can be judgements about the causes of failure that are inaccurate / distorted. The problem is that the original story teller (home / deputy manager) will have often left. I would argue that the question about the true causes of the service failing need to be robustly identified before formulating a solution.

Key Point 2 – which problems are symptoms, and which are underlying causes? This is very important as the underlying causes need disabling (no more fuel for a fire) otherwise the symptoms will simply morph into another form. This is where "swat teams" of highly competent managers sent into failing care homes and then leaving often don't work over the long term. This approach often focusses on symptoms (work to be done) rather than causes (need for greater staff engagement and the establishing of a credible home leader). You will need to be able to influence the underlying causes to have a good chance of a successful turnaround.

Provided these 2 key points have been successfully addressed we can move onto some qualifiers which increase the potential chances of success;

Qualifier 1 – does the service have foundations / or pockets of good practice? This may sound obvious but with an increasingly high bar in regulation, there needs to be some residual soundness in the service to build upon. For example, if there are problem supervisors, are there good carers? If the care plans are not good, is the care plan design ok, is it just a lack of training? The ability to drill down and isolate good practice gaps and create an action plan to fill them is the essence of a successful turnaround.

Qualifier 2 – regarding the ultimate organisational leader / nominated individual; Do they have the capacity, temperament and understanding to fulfil their responsibilities in running the service well? Can they meet their regulatory requirements?

Is the same person willing and able to fund the resources to support these responsibilities adequately?

Qualifier Point 3 – regarding larger homes - 70+beds or with several homes Have the directors previously worked in an environment with a large staff team, a well-developed management structure with defined roles, responsibilities devolved from the owner and the disciplines and accountability that come from such a structure?

Qualifier Point 4 – in terms of the leadership team (especially if friends or family of the owner in a small independent operator); Are the managers / directors self-aware – in terms of skills / required behaviours regarding their role?

Do they have previous experience in the sector to benchmark their own home / homes against?

Do they have an up to date knowledge of all legal and statutory frameworks which care homes work within and a firm commitment to honour the same?

Clearly this is a complex area, it resists generalisations and this article is far from exhaustive but hopefully identifies some of the variables that lead to dynamics which may have a bearing on whether it is possible to turn the service.

6.3 Reflective practice on **Care Home Manager / which services can be turned and which can't? Reflections from supporting an owner / operator.**

Key themes in this article

Breaking down the key points relating to failing services and identifying qualifiers for whether it is likely the service can be turned or not.

What does this article mean to you?

What can / would you apply from this learning to your practice?

Other notes

6.4 Care Home Manager / turning a blind eye / is it time you had that difficult conversation?

In our relationships with friends, family, it's normal and healthy to accept behaviours you don't like in another, it promotes understanding, it reflects a mature mind, it helps us to get past ourselves (ego) and see the world as it is. However, when you are leading a regulated service and it's a staff behaviour that you're observing that is contrary to established good practice, I put it to you that turning a blind eye can cause serious harm to your service. I want to make the case for you to now prepare to have that difficult conversation. Here's a case study for the same;

I managed a service in the south, working with a rather challenging young man who had been promoted beyond their level of competence. They were loud, abrasive and lacking competence with an exaggerated view of their ability. The team dynamics included low level bullying, fear and an absence of teamwork. Staff attrition was high, this leader had established a team of similar characters around him. Many good staff had left directly because of him yet they were still supported. I was told they were "bulletproof", and "untouchable". My problem was that this leader's behaviours were taking the focus away from the residents, ultimately leading to poor care. He meant well but he wasn't doing well. I knew I needed to deal with it. I knew if I did, it would get messy and it did!.

I heard various low level complaints but they weren't strong enough for me to get directly involved. I watched and as usual, the appropriate time came. The gentleman did a small thing wrong – shouted (being louder than normal he said), got angry, was overbearing (usual for them). Normally he apologies and brushes it off "It's just me, I won't do it again". This time, I framed the problem differently. I said that saying "this is just me" didn't absolve him from his responsibility to behave appropriately. As a manager, there were expected skills around communication, self-control, awareness of others and communication strategies required. He was experienced but not demonstrating these abilities. He later resigned and 7 others followed within a week. Fortunately, I was already working hard on recruitment, so within 5 weeks the vacant posts were covered. A couple of months later, the CQC visited the unit where this gentleman and team previously worked. They commented on the marked improvement in the culture, that it was more person-centred, the atmosphere had changed. I was pleased for the residents. It was worth it in the end. Let's break this down a bit more as it would be misleading to minimise the preparation involved and the risks taken to achieve this outcome;

After joining the home, I worked hard on recruitment as it had stalled. By doing this, I was less beholden to staff threatening to leave if they didn't "get their way". I wanted to keep the experienced and engaged staff and break the strange-hold of control from those wanted to run the home their way.

Next, I took 4 months to get a real sense of this character, a balanced view and to see whether their weaknesses were compensated by their strengths. It took a while to get beyond the evaluations and judgements. It took a while to discern that he was an impediment to the service and a root cause of team dysfunction.

Next was having the right intervention – which was to refuse to accept the behaviours. To suddenly say they didn't meet standards and to require ownership of the required behaviours for this role. This action became the catalyst and this is why I wanted to share this article with you. **The point was, he was doing the same behaviours for several years, this occasion was unexceptional. The difference was that I made a stand.** I applied the standards to his behaviour and required it. The point here is if you have a staff member habitually bending the (important) rules, with behaviours that weaken your home, even if you've overlooked it for years, **now is a good time to have that conversation**. Just because you accepted it then, doesn't preclude you from taking action now.

It takes guts to lead and not shy away from uncomfortable problems, to knowingly have uncomfortable conversations that will unsettle you and create tension but we always must keep in mind why we are doing it. We do it because our love for the residents exceeds our need to be comfortable and accepted. That's why we are leaders because we are trusted to do the right thing for those in our care.

Is it time you got ready for that difficult conversation?

6.4 Reflective practice on **Care Home Manager / turning a blind eye / is it time you had that difficult conversation?**

Key themes in this article

Making the connection between quality, leadership and well-planned, well executed (appropriate and balanced) difficult conversations.

What does this article mean to you?

What can / would you apply from this learning to your practice?

Other notes

6.5 Care Home Manager / vocation vs job / seeing the "giants" in our midst

I confess I've been a little quiet and to perfectly honest, my emotional reservoir DRIED UP a little! Not that you'd know, but I KNOW. It's subtle. I had some tough news, I was knocked back but not out. Emotionally I withdrew a little within to process, regroup, renew. It's healthy, a protection mechanism but left too long, it could become apathy.

To give my best, I need head and heart to be engaged. I was waiting, watching for the heart to awaken again. I recently visited a friend's care home at the weekend and saw this beautiful old couple; it was the look in the husband's eyes that spoke to me, touched me emotionally. It made me think deeply and I wanted to share that with you, just a moment to reflect;

His wife was bed-bound and seemed to lack capacity in the broad sense that we understand it. She was physically incapacitated as it were but he was just there. Held her hand. The look in his eyes was love; he was with the one he loved. As he turned his head and met my eyes, his eyes said he was the "cat that got the cream"! He was exactly where he wanted to be. He wasn't seeing what I briefly saw. There was no dementia or lack of capacity; he was with HIS WOMAN, likely HIS WIFE.

I don't know this person but I'd hazard a guess at a life of marriage (he was mid eighties by the looks of it). It appeared to be a continuance of a long relationship, from young people full of hope, promising to have to hold, no matter what, to be there, in sickness, in health, till death do us… What I loved about this gentleman was the love in his eyes for his wife, his dedication, his character in honouring that love and still loving.

It's hard to stay open to such small things around us I find. With a large home, team, residents, families, professionals, it is not always possible to notice these miracles, these giants in our midst, those who've done it all and live with love and courage to the very end. I don't say I never noticed before now but the greatness of this man's commitment touched me deeply. That he keep that deep love with his wife through the storms, ill health and just wanted to be with her. No doubt she could feel that presence, that love on some levels. It comforts me to think so. I had thought that these long suffering spouses were doing their duty, were coming to visit, to provide companionship but I hadn't thought deeply about someone just wanting and needing to be with the other is, just because they WANTED TO. It is love indeed.

I think the home manager is a true vocation and requires all that we are to really bring a sense of home, vitality, warmth and connection to the communities we lead and serve. It is easy to get lost in the tasks, the governance, the e mails and myriad of expectations and lose sight of the GIANTS in front of us. I know we can't always be so open, it's not practical but I am grateful that this man's love for his wife awakened me. With all my being, I endeavour to serve my team and residents with the best of me. They deserve that and to me a care home manager is always so much more than a job.

6.5 Reflective practice on **Care Home Manager / vocation vs. job / seeing the "giants" in our midst**

Key themes in this article

Vocation vs. a job. The emotional weight of working in social care and the need to manage our own emotions and self to stay engaged and effective. The value of familial bonds. The value of enduring love and loyalty between couples who've spent a lifetime together.

What does this article mean to you?

What can / would you apply from this learning to your practice?

Other notes

Beyond "**Leadership Secrets for Care Home Managers**"

If you want to continue the dialogue;

E mail me palmer.liamjdpalmer@gmail.com

For my latest projects and articles – see me via linked-in – if we're not already connected, do connect with me so we can learn together. I appreciate likes, comments on new material published via linked-in.

If you enjoyed this, may I ask a small favour?

Can I ask you to add a review to amazon – just a few sincere words will suffice. I may not be able to respond straight away but will respond to any messages I receive.

Wishing you continued success!

Liam Palmer

Birmingham, UK

Sep 2018

For further reading;

I also recommend the following by these social care visionaries and general good guys making a positive impact in the care home sector;

Neil Eastwood – "**Saving Social Care**"

Issac Theophilos - "**How to get outstanding. An ultimate guide for care homes.**"

Lightning Source UK Ltd.
Milton Keynes UK
UKHW020610080819
347620UK00016B/1731/P